COMPUTER
SCIENCE
UNLEASHED

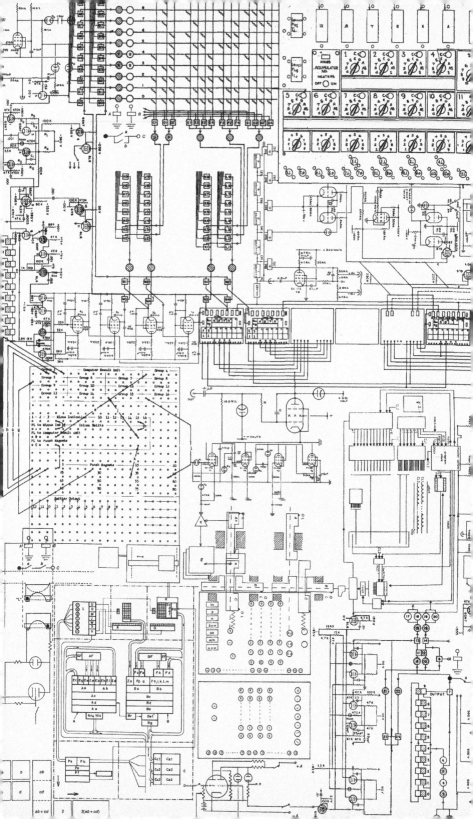

COMPUTER
SCIENCE
UNLEASHED

HARNESS THE POWER OF
COMPUTATIONAL SYSTEMS

WLADSTON FERREIRA FILHO
RAIMONDO PICTET

code energy

Las Vegas

©2021 Wladston Ferreira Filho and Raimondo Pictet

Published by CODE ENERGY, INC.

✉ hi@code.energy
🖥 http://code.energy
📷 http://instagram.com/code.energy
🐦 http://twitter.com/code_energy
👍 http://facebook.com/code.energy
🏠 304 S Jones Blvd # 401 Las Vegas NV 89107 🇺🇸

While every precaution has been taken in the preparation of this book, the publisher and the authors assume no responsibility for errors or omissions, or for damages resulting from the use of the information contained herein.

Publisher's Cataloging-in-Publication Data
Ferreira Filho, Wladston.
    Computer Science Unleashed: harness the power of computational systems / Wladston Ferreira Filho; with Raimondo Pictet. — 1st ed.
    x, 260 p. : il.
    ISBN 978-0-9973160-3-2 (Hardback)
    ISBN 978-0-9973160-4-9 (ebook)
1. Computer networks. 2. Internet. 3. Computer network protocols. 4. Regular expressions (computer science). 5. Statistics. 6. Data mining. 7. Machine learning. I. Title.
004 – dc22   2020925732

First Edition, December 2022.

To our friends Christophe and Mateus, one of whom bet we would finish this book by the end of the year.

Computer science has a lot in common with physics. Both are about how the world works at a rather fundamental level. The difference is that while in physics you're supposed to figure out how the world is made up, in computer science you create the world. In mathematics, as in programming, anything goes as long as it's self-consistent. You can have a set of equations in which three plus three equals two. You can do anything you want.

—LINUS TORVALDS
Explaining where his love for computers stems from.

CONTENTS

PREFACE

> I never liked the term 'computer science'. The main reason I don't like it is that there's no such thing. Computer science is a grab bag of tenuously related areas thrown together by an accident of history, like Yugoslavia.
>
> —PAUL GRAHAM

Most technological breakthroughs of our era are taking place in a new digital world created by programmers. Computer scientists combine different fields of study in order to empower this new world. This book explores the foundations of some of these fields, including networking, cryptography, and data science.

We'll start with the story of how two computers can be linked to share information, and take you all the way to the rise of email and the Web. We'll explore cryptography and understand how the Internet and other systems that deal with private data are made secure. Then, we'll learn how knowledge can be obtained from raw data and how machines can be taught to forecast the future.

We hope these stories will familiarize you with important concepts that can benefit coders and tech enthusiasts alike. Our goal is to cover what beginners need in order to get up to speed in networking, security and data science, without the heavy academic rigor that sometimes makes these topics unbearable.

Figure 1 "Data is the new oil", by Amit Danglé & Ivano Nardacchione.

This book was made possible by the supporters of our previous title, *Computer Science Distilled*. We had written our first book to explain the fundamental principles of computer science. Our enthusiastic readers asked for more, so we got back to work! This time, we don't explore the core of our discipline, but rather the new worlds it has enabled us to create.

Is this book for me?

If you're a novice programmer, this book was written for you. It doesn't require any programming experience, as it essentially presents ideas and mechanisms: we want you to learn how cool stuff works. If you're curious and want to understand how the Internet is built, how hackers attack computer systems, or why data is the gold of the 21st century, you'll find this book worthwhile. And for those who already studied computer science, this book is a great recap to consolidate your knowledge and expertise.

Acknowledgments

We are deeply grateful for everyone who supported our multi-year effort to create this book. We would especially like to thank Abner Marciano, André Lambert, Caio Magno, Carlotta Fabris, Damian Hirsch, Daniel Stori, Eduardo Barbosa, Gabriel Pictet, Guilherme Mattar, Jacqueline Wilson, Leonardo Conegundes, Lloyd Clark, Michael Ullman, Rafael Almeida, Rafael Viotti, and Ruhan Bidart. Finally, we're grateful to Claire Martin, our proofreader, and Pedro Netto, our illustrator, for making this book so much better.

May you create many worlds,
Wlad & Moto

Chapter 1

Connections

This is an entirely distributed system, there isn't any central control. The only reason it works is because everybody decided to use the same set of protocols.
—Vint Cerf

H UMANS CRAVE CONNECTIONS, and the advent of the digital revolution has empowered us to be more connected than ever before. The Internet has unleashed upon billions of people unprecedented economic and political freedom, as well as powerful means of control and domination. Yet, the vast majority of us are oblivious to its inner workings.

Skilled people who can program computers to use the Internet are at the vanguard of the digital revolution. This chapter will teach you how the Internet works, so you can join this select group. You'll learn to:

- 🔗 **Link** computers to one another to make a network,
- 🌐 Combine networks using the **Internet** Protocol,
- 📍 Locate a recipient from its Internet **address**,
- 🧭 Find a **route** through the Internet to that location,
- 🚚 **Transport** data between distant applications.

Before the Internet came along, telecommunication between two parties required a direct physical link. In the 1950s, each telephone had a wire leading directly to a central station. For a call to go through, an operator had to physically connect the wires of two telephones. For long distance calls, wires were laid out between distant stations, and several operators in different places had to physically connect the chain of wires linking the two phones.

The Internet did away with this. Wires aren't physically reconfigured to create direct, exclusive links. Instead, the information is retransmitted step by step via a chain of linked devices until it reaches its destination. This eliminates the need for wire operators and central coordination. Also, wires are no longer constrained to serve a single connection—many concurrent connections can share the same wire. This allows global communications to be instant, cheap and accessible.

However, modern networking technology is more intricate than early telephony. It has many successive layers, each building on top of the previous. Let's explore how connections are made at these different levels, starting with the most basic layer.

1.1 Links

A direct connection between two computers is achieved through a **transmission medium**: a physical channel where signals can flow. This may be a copper wire carrying electric currents, a fiber-optic cable directing light, or air hosting radio waves. Each connected computer has a **network interface** to send and receive signals in the transmission medium. For instance, cellphones have a radio chip and antenna to handle radio signals traveling through the air.

Figure 1.1 A **link** is established between two network interfaces if they share a transmission medium and agree on the rules of communication.

In order to communicate, network interfaces must agree on the rules to follow when sending and receiving signals. This set of rules is called the **link layer**.

When a medium *exclusively* connects two computers, we say they maintain a point-to-point connection, and their link layer relies on the most basic set of rules: the **Point-to-Point-Protocol** (**PPP**). It merely ensures the two computers can identify each other and exchange data accurately.

However, connected computers don't always get to enjoy such an exclusive link. Often, they must share the transmission medium with several other computers.

Shared Links

One way to link computers in an office is to plug each of them into a hub with a wire. The hub physically connects all the wires that reach it, so a signal sent by one computer will be detected by *all* the others! This will also happen on your home WiFi, since the same radio frequency is used by all connected devices. Communications can become messy if all of them use the medium at the same time.

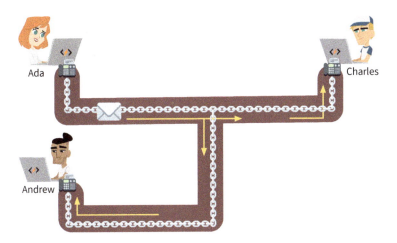

Figure 1.2 A message sent on a shared link will be detected by all.

The link layer contains a set of rules to define how computers should share their communication medium, fittingly called **Medium Access Control** (**MAC**). The rules resolve two main challenges:

COLLISIONS If two computers send a signal through the same medium at the same time, the resulting interference garbles both transmissions. Such events are called **collisions**. A similar problem occurs when your group of friends or family talk over each other and no single voice can be clearly heard.

There are methods to avoid collisions. First, only start transmitting signals when no other computer is transmitting. Second, monitor your communications—if a collision occurs, wait for a brief but random amount of time before trying to transmit again.

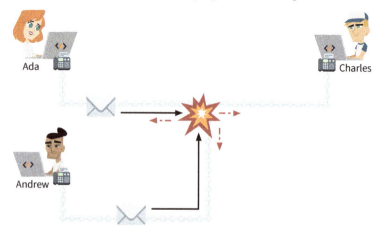

Figure 1.3 Collision between Ada and Andrew.

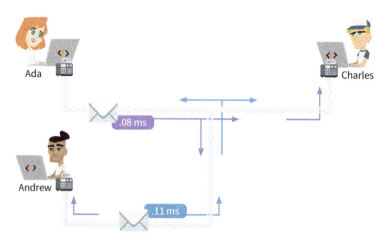

Figure 1.4 Ada and Andrew both resend after a random duration.

These methods have some limitations. When there are too many transmission attempts through a medium, collisions occur relentlessly. We say the link is **saturated** when excessive collisions break down communications. Have you ever been frustrated at a large venue because your phone wouldn't send text messages or make calls? This may happen if too many phones are attempting to communicate concurrently and the cellular link becomes saturated.

PHYSICAL ADDRESSING Ada and Charles have a direct link between their computers. Ada wants to talk with Charles, so she transmits a signal with her message through the medium. However, the medium is shared, so everyone linked to the medium gets the message. How can the other computers know that the signal they picked up was not destined for them?

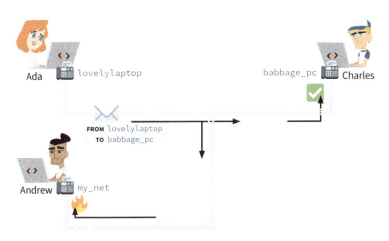

Figure 1.5 Andrew's network interface discards the message.

Each computer's network interface has an identifier, known as its **physical address** or **hardware address**. A transmission in a shared medium must begin with two such addresses: that of the recipient and that of the sender. Upon receiving a transmission, a computer will know if it should be ignored or picked up and to which address it should reply.

This can only work if physical addresses are unique: if two computers use "`my_netinterface`", we're back to square one. For this reason, virtually all network interfaces follow a naming scheme defined in the rules of Medium Access Control. These standard physical addresses are called **MAC addresses**.

MAC Addressing

Computers, smartphones, smart watches, and smart televisions can each have WiFi, Bluetooth, and Ethernet network interfaces. Each network interface has its own, unique MAC address marked into the hardware during production. You should not worry about assigning a MAC address to your computer: you can always use the one that came with its network interface.

Since MAC addresses are simply large random-looking numbers, network interface manufacturers around the world must coordinate to avoid accidentally assigning the same number to two different devices. To this end, they rely on the Institute of Electrical and Electronics Engineers, or **IEEE**, which assigns each of them a different range of MAC addresses.

A MAC address is expressed as six pairs of hexadecimals[1] separated by colons. The first half of the address is an identifier assigned by the IEEE to a unique manufacturer. This manufacturer then chooses a unique second half for each network interface.

`60:8B:0E:C0:62:DE`

Here, `608B0E` is the manufacturer number. This specific number was assigned by IEEE to Apple, so this MAC address should belong to an Apple device.[2] A device's MAC address is often written on a label stuck to the packaging or on the device itself, next to the serial number.

---

[1] In day-to-day life, we almost always express numbers in decimal form, where each digit is one of ten characters: 0, 1, 2, 3, 4, 5, 6, 7, 8, 9. Computer scientists, on the other hand, like expressing numbers in hexadecimal form, where each digit can be one of sixteen characters: 0, 1, 2, 3, 4, 5, 6, 7, 8, 9, a, b, c, d, e, f. For more about number bases, see Appendix I.

[2] You can look up who manufactured a device by entering the first six digits of its MAC address at http://code.energy/mac-lookup.

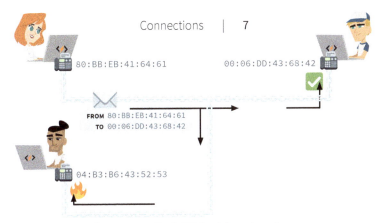

Figure 1.6   Each MAC address is unique.

There's a special address reserved for transmissions to all computers in a medium. It's called the **broadcast address**, and it reads `FF:FF:FF:FF:FF`. You use it when you try to connect to an unknown device. For instance, when your smartphone's WiFi card isn't deactivated, it persistently broadcasts to `FF:FF:FF:FF:FF` that it's looking for an access point. Discoverable access points will respond with their own MAC address so you can establish a link.

Such discovery broadcasts, like all other transmissions, contain the sender's MAC address. Walking around with a smartphone can therefore be like walking around with a loudspeaker shouting your name non-stop, only using radio waves instead of sound and the MAC address instead of your moniker. In 2013, Edward Snowden revealed that the NSA[3] monitored the movements of people by sniffing WiFi transmissions in big cities, storing records of where each MAC address was seen.

You can also set your own network interface to **promiscuous mode**, and it will pick up all transmissions regardless of their intended recipient. Doing so allows you to discover hidden WiFi networks, to list which MAC addresses are in your area, and sometimes even to read the contents of other people's transmissions. Browsing the Internet through an unsecured WiFi network can therefore be unsafe: anyone in range can hear what you broadcast. This is why encryption[4] is important for WiFi's link layer.

Be careful: a network interface can be configured for its transmissions to start with any MAC address both for the recipient *and*

---

[3]National **S**ecurity **A**gency, a US government spying organization.
[4]Encryption allows messages to look garbled to eavesdroppers.

for the sender. Nothing stops a malicious agent from impersonating you by using your physical address in their transmissions. This type of attack is known as **MAC spoofing**. When the link layer was originally developed, security wasn't a concern. Protocols are evolving to become more secure and neutralize such attacks, but it's an ongoing process.

Frames

Sometimes, a transmission must contain a lot of data, and sending out a single, big fat message is impractical. Network interfaces and computers are not all capable of the same transmission speeds. Moreover, what would happen if a collision occurred in the middle of the transmission? The entire transmission would have to be discarded, as it would be difficult for the sender and receiver to determine exactly which parts of the message were received and which were not.

To solve these issues, long messages are always split into small parts, each sent as an independent transmission. The time between transmissions can vary according to the capabilities of both computers: slower devices need longer breaks. If an error occurs, it is only necessary to discard and resend the small transmission that failed.

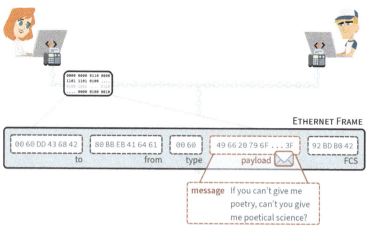

Figure 1.7 An Ethernet frame. Once it is transmitted in a copper wire, it becomes a series of electric signals that encode a number. The Ethernet protocol instructs how to interpret this number. For instance, the first 12 hex digits of the number encode the destination MAC address.

Each independent transmission is called a **frame**. Standard WiFi protocols cap the size of frames to 2,346 bytes. Thirty-four bytes are needed for MAC addresses and error-detecting codes. Therefore, a WiFi frame can ultimately carry up to 2,312 bytes of data, called the payload.[5] In wired networks, the maximum frame size is usually 1,526 bytes, with room for a 1,500 byte payload.

On rare occasions, disturbances in the medium interfere with a transmission, and the receiver picks up signals that don't encode exactly the same information that the sender intended to transmit. Let's see the special field that was added to address this problem.

FCS   The last part of the frame is the **FCS** (**F**rame **C**heck **S**equence), and it ensures that information was transmitted accurately. The FCS doesn't add new information to the transmission: it is merely the result of a calculation using the contents of all other fields. Changing any content before the FCS should cause the FCS number to change as well.

Upon receiving a frame, a computer calculates the *expected* FCS number from the information it received and compares it to the *received* FCS. If they don't match, the frame is discarded. If they match, we know that the message wasn't garbled and trust that the received payload is error-free.

TYPE   The frame shown in Figure 1.7 has one last field we haven't talked about: the payload **type**. It tells the receiver which rules should be followed to interpret the data in the frame's payload. In the next section, we'll explore the most common set of such rules.

1.2   Internet

We've seen that the link layer enables directly connected computers to exchange messages inside frames. The **internet layer**, also known as the **network layer**, specifies how to transmit these messages between computers that are *not* directly connected.

The trick is to equip some computers, called **routers**, with multiple network interfaces. All computers in a network are then linked

---

[5]If we encode one byte per character, a WiFi frame has room for about 500 words, enough to fill a page of text.

to at least one router, and all routers are linked to at least one other router. When a router receives a message at one of its network interfaces, it can forward it to another router through a different network interface.

LOCAL AREA NETWORKS We can ask a router we're linked with to forward a message to a computer we're not linked with. Suppose you have a wired network in your home connecting a router and a desktop computer. Suppose the router is also directly connected to a smartphone in a different, wireless network.

Even though the desktop computer and the smartphone are not directly connected to the same network, they can send messages to each other using the router as a relay. Computers from different networks in close vicinity that can talk to each other through routers form a larger network, called a Local Area Network (**LAN**).

In a home or small office, one router will be enough to link all the computer networks in the area. When assembling a LAN that covers a large organization such as a university or hospital, many routers may be required to link all the different computers networks into a fully connected system.

Figure 1.8 In this small LAN, Ada and Andrew can send messages to each other through their router Charles.

WIDE AREA NETWORKS But why stop there? If your router is linked with a router outside your home, which in turn is linked with a router at the university, you can ask for your message to be forwarded to computers on the university's LAN. When distant LANs are connected to each other, they form a Wide Area Network (**WAN**).

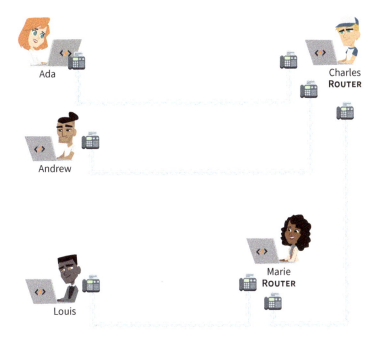

Figure 1.9 Charles is connected to a distant router, Marie, and they both forward messages around this WAN.

A WAN can grow larger as more LANs are connected to it. Different WANs can also be connected to form an even larger WAN. The largest WAN in the world is a collection of thousands of **inter**connected **net**works that we call **the Internet**. It's the network we use every day to send emails and browse the web; and as of 2020, it contained over a billion computers. Let's see how they all got connected.

Interconnection

The most straightforward way to connect your router to the Internet is to pay for it. Some organizations on the Internet will link one of their routers to yours, and allow messages to and from your network to pass through their network via this link. This paid service is called **transit**, as all of your messages will *transit* through their network before going to the specific router you're aiming for.

However, transiting through a third party network is not always necessary in order to connect to another router of the Internet. Say, for example, that two nearby universities communicate a lot; they can link their routers in order for messages to flow directly between their networks. This can save money, as these messages would otherwise have to transit through a paid connection. The free exchange of messages between the networks of different organizations is called **peering**.

Routing

Any computer linked to a router of the Internet can ask for its messages to be forwarded by other routers. Messages can be routed over large distances. For instance, there is a system of submarine cables linking routers in many coastal cities:

Figure 1.10 The SAm-1 system links routers in 16 cities from 11 different countries, using over 15 thousand miles of underwater cables.

There is no direct link between the routers in Miami and Buenos Aires. However, Miami is linked with Puerto Rico, which is itself linked with Fortaleza, which is linked with Rio de Janeiro, which is finally linked with Buenos Aires. Miami and Buenos Aires can exchange messages through these cables if routers along the way forward them back and forth. Today, there are submarine cables linking hundreds of coastal city routers around the globe:

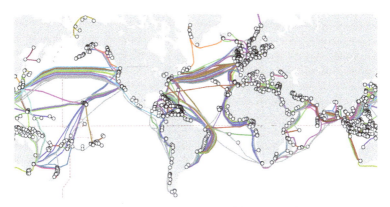

Figure 1.11   Fiber-optic submarine cables currently in service.

Virtually every other city on Earth is directly or indirectly linked to these coastal cities, often through cables in the ground. Communication satellites also have routers to establish wireless links to remote locations. All routers can forward messages, so a message you send on the Internet can be routed to any other computer on the Internet. That is, *if* a path to it can be found.

Location Addressing

In the link layer, computers are identified by a physical address. Physical addresses uniquely identify computers, but they don't give any hints on *where* a computer is connected and how it can be reached. If the computer moves to the other side of the world, it will retain its physical address!

Suppose you mailed a package to Louis through the post along with a picture of him instead of his address. This package has a defined destination; however, an international postal service would have no way of knowing which direction the package should be sent in order to deliver it to Louis.

Post offices must first know to which country the package should go. The first post office in that country should then know to which province or state it should go. The next post office should know the city, and the final post office, the street address. We call an address containing all this information a **hierarchical address**. Similarly to post offices, routers require packages to carry a hierarchical address of their recipient's location:

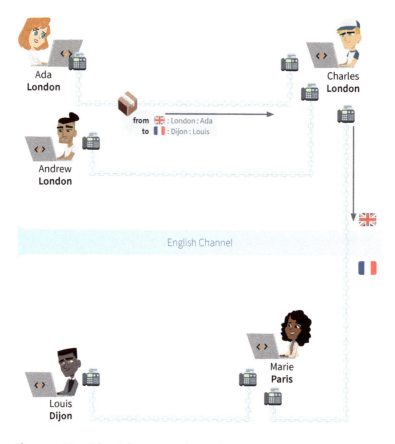

Figure 1.12 Ada wishes to send a package to Louis, so she requests her router Charles to forward it. She writes on the package a hierarchical address of Louis. Charles then knows he must send the package to France, so he sends it to the French router he is linked with: Marie.

For this mechanism to work on a global scale, *all* computers involved must follow the same set of rules to create and handle package forwarding requests. A computer in China must understand a request from a computer in Nigeria, even though the two may use different languages, operating systems and hardware.

Figure 1.13 "Before the Internet", courtesy of http://xkcd.com.

Internet Protocol

We've seen a computer must follow the rules of Medium Access Control to establish a link with another computer. Similarly, it must follow the **Internet Protocol**, or **IP**,[6] to ask routers to forward messages to other computers on your LAN or on the Internet.

A message forwarding request that follows the IP rules is called an **IP packet**. The IP packet is essentially a big number, where digits in specific positions encode key information. Almost every computer produced in the past few decades understands IP packets and is able to forward them. This makes an IP packet easily movable from one computer to the next, until it reaches its destination.

An IP packet contains the *location* addresses of its sender and recipient, followed by whatever data they want. To send an IP packet, we transmit a frame where the payload is the IP packet, and the frame type is **86DD**. When a router receives a frame of this type, the IP packet is re-transmitted in another frame to the next computer in the path of the packet's destination.

---

[6]By "IP", we mean its latest version, **IPv6**. A legacy version of the protocol, **IPv4**, is still used, despite being released in 1981. IPv4 can only support about 3 billion computers. IPv6, launched in 2012, can support a virtually unlimited number of computers. As of 2020, a third of the Internet's computers use IPv6.

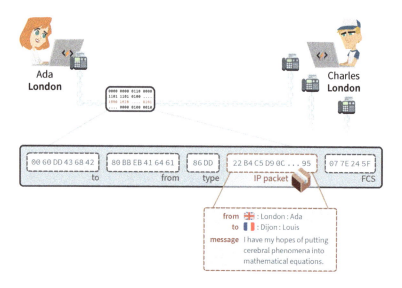

Figure 1.14 Ada sends an Ethernet frame to her router Charles containing an IP packet for Louis. The Ethernet frame therefore contains the physical address of Charles and the packet contains the location address of Louis. Charles will then forward the packet inside a new frame of his own containing the physical address of someone in France.

In order for IP packets to be forwarded around universally, everybody must agree on a standard for location addressing. We've seen how physical addresses are allocated by manufacturers according to the rules of Medium Access Control. Let's now learn how the Internet Protocol does this for location addresses. We will then see how the Internet Protocol defines routing rules based on these addresses.

1.3   IP Addressing

The Internet Protocol sets the rules on how location addresses work—that's why they're called **IP addresses**. Computers can only send or receive IP packets after they get an IP address. Permission to use a group of IP addresses is first granted to an organization. These addresses are then assigned to computers which are directly or indirectly associated with the organization.

In order to explain how this process works, let's define what IP addresses are and how they're written.[7] An IP address is a number 128 bits long.[8] They're typically written in hex, with colons separating eight groups of four digits. This is Facebook server's IP address:

```
2a03:2880:f003:0c07:face:b00c:0000:0002
```

IP addresses can be shortened by omitting the leading zeros of any four-digit block:

```
2a03:2880:f003:c07:face:b00c::2
```

As with a postal address with country, city and street, IP addresses are hierarchical for routing to be possible. While the broadest part of a postal address is the country, the broadest part of an IP address is the **routing prefix**:

2a03:2880:f003:c07:face:b00c::2

routing prefix

The prefix shows up as the first digits of an IP address. Once an organization is granted such a prefix, it has the right to assign any IP address that begins with that prefix to its computers. The prefix has a variable length: organizations that have more computers to manage are granted shorter prefixes. Some organizations are even granted multiple prefixes.

For example, we know that all addresses that begin with the prefix **2a03:2880** are assigned to computers inside Facebook's network. Those that begin with **2c0f:fb50:4002** are in Google's network in Kenya. For its data center in Singapore, Google was granted the prefix **2404:6800**.

For routing purposes, the LANs and WANs that share the same prefix are organized in small networks called **subnets**. The digits

---

[7]We'll present IP addresses as defined in the latest version of IP. Legacy IPv4 addresses are still used. They are written as four groups of up to three digit decimal numbers, separated by dots, for example, 192.168.0.1.

[8]It takes 128 zeros and ones to write the number. This means it's a number between 0 and 340,282,366,920,938,463,463,374,607,431,768,211,456.

after the routing prefix and up to the middle of an IP address indicate in which subnet a computer can be found.

`2a03:2880:`f003:c07`:face:b00c::2`

subnet

This means there's a network at Facebook where all computers have IP addresses that begin with `2a03:2880:f003:c07`. Together, the routing prefix and the subnet form the **network ID** of an IP address. The network ID is always 16 digits long (including omitted zeros). This means an organization with a longer routing prefix can have less subnets within it.

Finally, the next 16 digits of an IP address are called the **interface ID**, as they identify a specific network interface within a subnet. Many network administrators simply fill in this part of the IP address with the device's MAC address. These digits can be any number, as long as it's only used once per subnet.

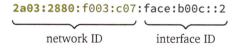

`2a03:2880:f003:c07:face:b00c::2`

network ID   interface ID

For this addressing system to work universally, there must be a mechanism to ensure no two organizations use the same routing prefix. As was the case for MAC addresses, engineers solved this through some international coordination.

Figure 1.15 Don't ask your boss where she lives!

IANA

Engineers worldwide agreed that an American non-profit organization, the Internet Assigned Numbers Authority (**IANA**), decides who gets control over which IP routing prefixes. In practice, IANA delegates most of its power to five non-profit organizations called Regional Internet Registries, or **RIR**s. To do so, it allocates each RIR short hex combinations that they can use as the first digits of the routing prefixes they assign.

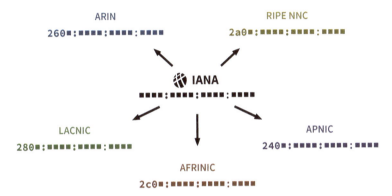

Figure 1.16   Examples of allocations to each RIR.

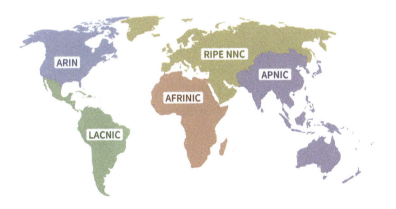

Figure 1.17   IANA delegates its IP addressing power geographically: each RIR is responsible for a different region.

To obtain a routing prefix for your organization, you must make a request to the RIR of the region where your routers will be. That RIR will then assign you a prefix starting with one of their combinations of hex digits that IANA allocated them.

For example, Facebook, which has headquarters in Ireland, was granted its routing prefix by RIPE NCC. Likewise, the Swiss bank Credit Suisse has a Latin American branch that was granted a routing prefix by LACNIC:

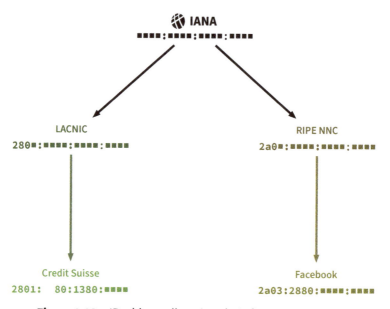

Figure 1.18 IP address allocation chain for two companies.

This means computers in the Latin American Credit Suisse branches may be assigned IP addresses as follows:

```
2801:80:1380:████:____:____:____:____
```

Network administrators in the bank will assign a unique combination of hex digits to each of their subnets such that they fit in the remaining space of the network part ████. Since each hex digit can have 16 different values, the bank has enough space for $16^4 = 65,536$ different subnets. Facebook, being a larger organization, was granted a prefix with room for over 4 billion subnets!

We've seen that network administrators can choose how the sixteen blanks of the interface ID are to be filled for individual devices. Such devices may then send and receive IP packets to and from the Internet as long as their router has connectivity.

Internet Service Providers

Most individuals and small organizations don't deal directly with RIRs, nor do they maintain peering links to other computer networks. Instead, they buy Internet connectivity from specialized companies, which are called Internet Service Providers (**ISP**). ISPs install routers close to their customers. That way, they can easily link one of their routers to a router in any customer's premises. They also allocate a routing prefix for each of their customers.

Let's see how it works in practice. In the United Kingdom, an ISP called Sky was granted the routing prefix `2a02:0c7f`. Sky operates in many British cities, so the prefix is divided between their regional bases. For instance, they assign `2a02:c7f:48` to their Milton Keynes network and `2a02:c7f:7e` to the one in Romford.[9]

Let's suppose Ada lives in Romford and wants to set up a network in her home. She has a desktop computer and a printer which she wants to connect using an Ethernet wire. She also wants her own WiFi network to connect her smartphone, tablet and laptop.

Ada hires Sky, and they link their Romford router to a router in her home. Sky assigns Ada's router a 14-digit routing prefix based on the one of their Romford base. Each network in Ada's home (wired and wireless) gets assigned a subnet, based on the routing prefix Sky allocated to Ada. Figure 1.19 on the next page shows the full IP address allocation path from IANA to each of Ada's devices.

Ada's router receives IP packets from several different computers, yet it's easy for her router to decide on which link to forward each packet it receives. Packets addressed to a computer in one of Ada's subnets can be directly delivered. All other IP packets it receives are forwarded through the link to the ISP.

---

[9]This information is public, you can look up the network location of any routing prefix. The practice is called **IP geolocation**, and it's how websites guess the country and city you browse from.

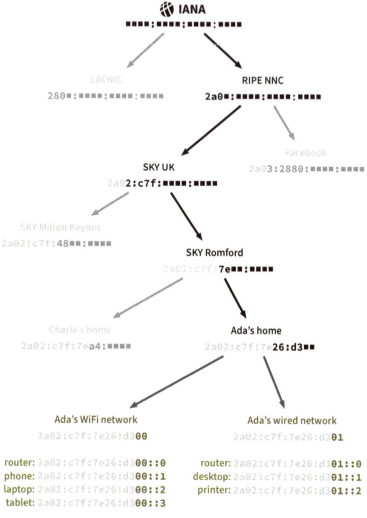

Figure 1.19 IP address allocations from IANA to Ada's devices. Her router uses different subnets for her wireless and wired networks, and therefore has a different IP address for each.

For routers that don't rely on an ISP, it's not so easy: they obtain connectivity from links with several routers from multiple computer networks. But how do they decide on which link they should forward an IP packet? And even then, how can they be sure that they are forwarding it to a router closer to their final destination?

1.4 IP Routing

Suppose Ada wants to send a message to Facebook from her laptop. She will use the Internet Protocol, so she starts by crafting an IP packet that includes her own IP address, Facebook's IP address, and her message as the payload. She then transmits the packet in a WiFi frame from her laptop to her home router:

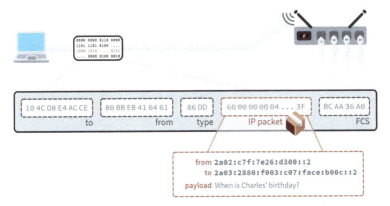

Figure 1.20 An IP packet transmitted over WiFi.[10]

Several routers, starting with the one at Ada's home, retransmit the packet until it reaches Facebook. Along the way, each of those routers must choose in which direction the packet should "hop" to reach the next router. The last router will then make the packet "hop" towards its final destination computer.

Tables of Addresses

Routers choose the next hop of a packet based on its destination IP address. In order to do so, they are equipped with a table filled with IP addresses. Rows list possible addresses the router is configured to recognize. For each address, the table indicates which computer should be the next hop of a packet destined to that address. Every router has a unique table that reflects how the router is linked. For example, here is how Ada's router is linked:

---

[10]We've included the fields of the WiFi frame which also exist in Ethernet frames. A WiFi frame has more fields, which were hidden for simplicity.

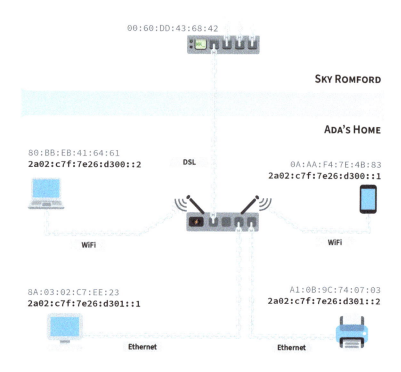

Figure 1.21 Ada's router is connected to a desktop computer and a printer via Ethernet, a notebook and a smartphone via WiFi, and to the ISP via DSL (or *Digital Subscriber Line*, a technology that allows digital data to flow through old telephone cables).

Destination IP address	Interface	MAC address
2a02:c7f:7e26:d301::1	Ethernet	8A:03:02:C7:EE:23
2a02:c7f:7e26:d301::2	Ethernet	A1:0B:9C:74:07:03
2a02:c7f:7e26:d300::1	WiFi	0A:AA:F4:7E:4B:83
2a02:c7f:7e26:d300::2	WiFi	80:BB:EB:41:64:61
default	DSL	00:60:DD:43:68:42

Figure 1.22 Table that guides Ada's router to correctly forward IP packets to computers shown in Figure 1.21.

If the router receives a packet whose destination IP address doesn't match any row in the table, the packet is forwarded through to the **default route**. For Ada's router, routing is simple: a packet is either directly delivered to a computer in her home or forwarded to Sky Romford, her ISP.

Routing is more complicated for the ISP's router. In addition to its peering and transit links, it receives packets from many different customers. For simplicity, let's suppose Sky Romford's router only serves two customers and has two peering links: one to the Sky router in Milton Keynes, and the other to Oxford University. Finally, let's imagine it has a transit link with a larger telecom company:

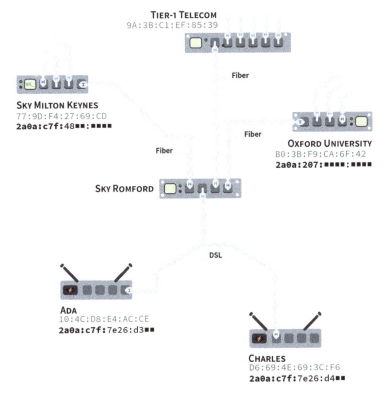

Figure 1.23 Map of Sky Romford links. Ada, Charles, and Oxford University can talk using Sky's local infrastructure only.

Destination IP address	Interface	MAC address
2a0a:c7f:7e26:d3■■:…	DSL	10:4C:D8:E4:AC:CE
2a0a:c7f:7e26:d4■■:…	DSL	D6:69:4E:69:3C:F6
2a0a:c7f:48■■:■■■■:…	Fiber	77:9D:F4:27:69:CD
2a0a:207:■■■■:■■■■:…	Fiber	B0:3B:F9:CA:6F:42
default	Fiber	9A:3B:C1:EF:85:39

Figure 1.24 Table that guides Sky Romford's router to correctly forward IP packets to networks shown in Figure 1.23.

This is where the IP addressing hierarchy comes in handy. In the forwarding table of fig. 1.24, IP addresses are grouped according to their routing prefix. This works because all IP addresses starting with **2a0a:207** are from computers in Oxford University, and all IP addresses starting with **2a02:c7f:48** are from computers serviced by Sky in Milton Keynes.

Internet Exchange Points

In order to increase capacity and speed, network administrators often set up peering links with as many other organizations as possible. The cheapest way to do this is through places called **Internet Exchange Points**, or **IXPs**. Organizations join an IXP by wiring their routers to the IXP building. Every participating organization can then establish individual peering links with other organizations connected to the building.[11]

In fig. 1.23, only two peering links were shown for clarity's sake. A typical ISP actually has scores of peering links per IXP they're wired to. In addition, it's common in big cities for Internet corporations like Netflix and Google to establish peering links directly with ISPs, allowing them shorter and faster connections to many of their customers.

---

[11]IXPs are extremely important for making the Internet well connected and cheap. This video explains why: http://code.energy/IXP.

Internet Backbone

ISPs and other telecom companies typically expand their interconnections as much as possible by establishing peering links wherever they can. However, in order to reach networks they cannot peer with, they have to buy transit from other operators.

There is a handful of companies in the world that don't pay anyone for transit. These companies operate *huge* networks that all peer with each other, allowing regional ISPs to be interconnected globally. These *huge* networks are called **Tier-1 networks**, and they form the backbone of the Internet. Some of them are operated by AT&T, Verizon, and Lumen.[12]

Dynamic Routing

Large telecom companies must maintain connectivity even if some of their transit or peering links break down. This means that they can't rely on a single link for each routing prefix in their table of addresses. In fact, they have **dynamic routers** that map out how other networks are interconnected in order to choose which routes to prioritize in their tables.

Dynamic routers periodically exchange information with other dynamic routers they're linked to. They tell each other which network prefixes are reachable through each of their links. This allows them to determine how many hops away each link is from every routing prefix and where these hops occur. Dynamic routers can then determine the best route to each prefix based on metrics like distance and speed.[13]

With this information, dynamic routers build a table that covers all routing prefixes. For each prefix, the table indicates which next hop is on the best route to the final destination. When a link is established or a link goes down, dynamic routers inform their peers. As the news spreads, all of them update their tables to keep forwarding packets towards the best routes.

---

[12]For an idea of how colossal these networks are, Lumen alone manages and operates 750,000 miles of fiber optic cables. That's more than enough cable to reach the moon, *three times!*

[13]All five RIRs constantly disclose information on all routing prefixes they delegate. Dynamic routers closely track these announcements, so they can ensure their tables have a row for every existing routing prefix.

There is no central entity coordinating the exchange of this information: routers share link details with their peers freely and voluntarily. Consequently, routing problems often emerge.

Routing Loop

Misconfigured routers can provoke errors. Most notably, bugged tables of addresses can send a packet *back* a few hops, and it gets caught in an endless cycle of doom:

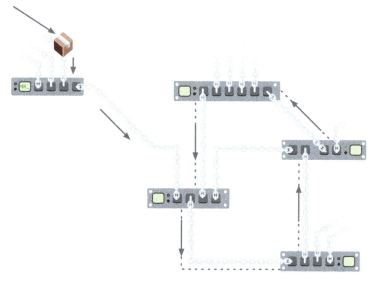

Figure 1.25   Bugged tables sending a packet round in circles.

If the tables aren't corrected, more packets with the same intended destination will be endlessly forwarded in circles. Too many packets can even saturate and clog the links. This is known as a **routing loop problem**. Fortunately, the Internet Protocol provides a way to identify the issue when it occurs.

HOP LIMIT   To interrupt perpetual routing loops, all IP packets carry a **hop limit** between 0 and 255. It indicates the number of times the packet can be forwarded by routers. Typically, packets are created with a hop limit of 64. Whenever a router forwards a packet, it reduces the hop limit by one:

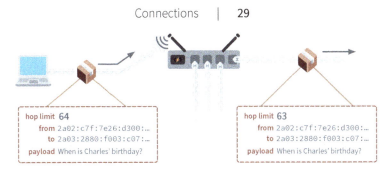

hop limit **64**
 from 2a02:c7f:7e26:d300:…
  to 2a03:2880:f003:c07:…
payload When is Charles' birthday?

hop limit **63**
 from 2a02:c7f:7e26:d300:…
  to 2a03:2880:f003:c07:…
payload When is Charles' birthday?

Figure 1.26 A packet's hop limit is the only element of an IP packet that routers change while forwarding.

If a packet is going around in circles, its hop limit will eventually reach zero. If a router receives an IP packet with a hop limit of zero, it can be discarded. An IP packet containing an error message should then be transmitted back to the sender by the last router, stating that the packet could not be delivered because its hop limit was reached.

Feedback through such error messages helps network administrators fix critical bugs, and routing loops are not the only ones. In fact, the Internet Protocol covers how a variety of routing problems should be dealt with.

Diagnostics

Routers discard IP packets that they are unable to handle. When this happens, they send an informational message about the incident to the packet's sender. The Internet Protocol defines how routers must format such messages, ensuring they can be understood by any computer. These rules are a subset of the Internet Protocol called the Internet Control Message Protocol (**ICMP**).

ICMP assigns error codes to the most common routing problems. To report a problem, a router sends an IP packet containing the error code as the message body, formatted according to ICMP rules. Let's see some common problems that can be reported using ICMP, starting with the routing loop problem.

TIME EXCEEDED If a router receives an IP packet with a hop limit of zero, its travel time is up. The packet either got stuck on a routing loop, or it was granted an insufficient hop limit by the sender.

In such cases, an ICMP message with a **time exceeded** error code is sent back. The ICMP message includes the first bytes of the discarded packet to allow the original sender to know which packet didn't make it to its destination.

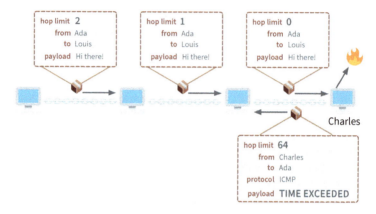

Figure 1.27   Once a router receives a packet with a hop limit of zero, it is discarded and an ICMP error message is sent to the packet's sender.

Notice that the IP packet Charles sends back in fig. 1.27 includes a protocol field. It's a two-digit hex number identifying how the packet's payload should be interpreted. The latest version of ICMP was assigned the protocol number 0x3A. All IP packets must include a protocol number. In the next section, we'll learn more about this. For now, let's explore other common routing problems.

DESTINATION UNREACHABLE Sometimes, a router has nowhere to send a packet. This can happen for many different reasons, for example if the IP address isn't in the router's table of addresses, and the table doesn't propose a default next hop. Sometimes, the next hop happens to be offline.

When the router doesn't know where to forward the packet, it returns an ICMP message with the **destination unreachable** error code, along with the first bytes of the discarded packet's content.

PACKET TOO BIG We've seen that link layer protocols limit the amount of data that can be sent in a single frame. Frames from different types of network links can carry payloads of different sizes.

The maximum number of payload bytes that can be carried in a single frame is called its **Maximum Transmission Unit** (**MTU**). Different link layer protocols have different MTU values. For Ethernet frames, the MTU is 1,500. For WiFi frames, it's 2,305.

If a router receives a larger packet than what the next hop can handle, it can't be forwarded as it stands. Instead, the router returns an ICMP message with the **packet too big** error code, the first bytes of the problematic packet, and the MTU of the next hop. The informed sender can then trim or split the original message into smaller packets before trying again.

Figure 1.28   "MTU", courtesy of Daniel Stori (http://turnoff.us).

PARAMETER PROBLEM An IP packet contains a lot of extra information alongside its payload. We've seen it contains IP addresses, a hop limit, and a protocol number. It also includes a field indicating the size of the payload and another specifying the version of the Internet Protocol it respects. Additional fields are also there to help routers prioritize important packets.

All these fields must be ordered and formatted according to strict rules. When a router receives a packet that doesn't conform to the protocol, it returns an ICMP message with the **parameter problem** error code and the location in the packet where the conflict was found. As usual, the ICMP message also contains a few bytes of the discarded packet for identification purposes.

INFORMATIONAL MESSAGES Error reports are not the only messages ICMP defines to inspect and diagnose faulty computer networks. Most notably, the **echo request** and **echo reply** informational message pair is widely utilized. When a computer receives an ICMP echo request, it returns a packet containing an ICMP echo reply.

This is useful to test if a computer is online. There's a program called `ping` that sends out an ICMP echo request message and measures how long it takes for the reply to reach you.[14] Furthermore, by sending ICMP echo requests with different initial hop limits, you can trace the route packets follow to reach their destination.[15]

1.5 Transport

We've seen that computers on the Internet can exchange messages in IP packet payloads. For example, they can exchange ICMP messages. However, the true power of the Internet is unleashed when *applications*, not computers, start sending each other data in IP packet payloads.

Computers on a network are often called **hosts** because they merely *host* the applications that utilize the network. For instance, a smartphone can host applications to simultaneously stream music, surf the web, and receive emails.

Generally, an application shares its host with other applications, but it doesn't want to go through all incoming IP packets. To solve this issue, applications ask their hosts to send and receive the packets on their behalf. That way, the hosts direct each packet's payload toward the right application, and each application only receives the data it should be reading.

This solution requires the data sent by an application to be accompanied by some extra information. The **transport layer** specifies how to format and interpret this extra information within an IP packet's payload.

---

[14]You can send ICMP packets here: http://code.energy/ping.

[15]An explanation of how ICMP is used to trace the routes IP packets travel through can be found at http://code.energy/traceroute.

User Datagram Protocol

The simplest transport layer protocol is the **User Datagram Protocol**, or **UDP**. Applications that use UDP are assigned **port numbers** by their hosts. Exchanged messages are preceded by the port numbers of both sending and receiving applications.

To communicate via UDP, an application first creates a **socket**. A socket is a communication channel between the application and its host. Suppose Facebook's server is running a calendar application using UDP port number 18. An application running on Ada's host can send a message to this hypothetical Facebook application as follows:

```
socket ← SOCKET.new(IP, UDP)
message ← "When is Charles' birthday?"
facebook_address ← 2a03:2880:f003:c07:face:b00c::2
app_port ← 18
socket.sendto(message, facebook_address, app_port)
```

When sending this message, Ada's host automatically assigns an unused port number to the newly created socket. Let's suppose that it selects the port number **54321**. The IP packet that's transmitted when **sendto()** is called will look like this:

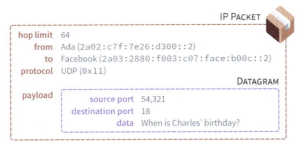

Figure 1.29 | hop limit | 64 |
from	Ada (2a02:c7f:7e26:d300::2)
to	Facebook (2a03:2880:f003:c07:face:b00c::2)
protocol	UDP (0x11)

DATAGRAM

payload	source port	54,321
destination port	18
data	When is Charles' birthday?

Figure 1.29 When an IP packet's payload conforms to the UDP format, it's called a **datagram**. Packets carrying datagrams have their protocol number set to **0x11**.

A host can manage thousands of different sockets for its applications. A single application can even create multiple sockets to operate many communication channels in parallel. Each socket gets assigned its own port number by its host.

Consider our hypothetical calendar application on Facebook's host. Upon receiving Ada's initial contact, it returns a datagram with destination port 54,321 in a packet for Ada's IP address. Ada's app waits for this datagram by calling another socket method:

```
received ← socket.recv()
```

This halts Ada's application until a datagram arrives at port 54,321. Once that happens, the incoming data is stored in received, and the application resumes.

CLIENT & SERVER For two applications to communicate, one must be waiting for contact and the other must initiate it. We call the former a **server**, and the latter a **client**. In our example, the Facebook application is the server and Ada's application is the client. However, Ada's application could also act as a server. It must simply create a socket, bind it to the port at which it expects to receive datagrams, and wait for contact:

```
socket ← Socket.new(IP, UDP)
socket.bind(17)
received ← socket.recv()
```

You select your server's port number. If another application in the host already has a socket bound to that port, bind() throws an error. When recv() is called, the application halts until a datagram bearing your port number arrives. Along with the datagram's data, the sender's IP address and source port number are stored in the received variable. This way, the application can choose to reply if it must:

```
received ← socket.recv()
x ← process_data(received.data)
socket.sendto(x, received.src_ip, received.src_port)
```

UDP CHECKSUM We've seen that every computer and router on a network can check the integrity of Ethernet and WiFi frames it receives thanks to their FCS field. A datagram inside an IP packet is carried on a different frame for each link, therefore the FCS changes at every hop. Unfortunately, this means there is no way for a host receiving a datagram to know if all these FCS have been properly generated and verified.

To address this issue, each datagram carries its own integrity checker called the **UDP checksum**. This checksum is only generated once and verified once, by its sending and receiving hosts respectively. Corrupted datagrams are automatically discarded by the receiving host, so its applications can trust incoming data has not been accidentally damaged.

UDP LIMITATIONS A datagram must be short enough to fit inside the payload of one IP packet. Since the MTU for the bulk of the Internet is 1,500 bytes, most datagrams are designed to respect that limit. A heavy message, such as a large photo, must be sent through multiple IP packets.

Recall that any IP packet may hit an overloaded router in its path and be dropped. Sometimes, hosts are not even notified when their packets disappear. Furthermore, packet handling by routers can cause them to arrive disordered or duplicated. This makes it difficult to recover data that is split in multiple datagrams.

UDP is best suited for applications whose requests and replies fit in one datagram each. Ideally, an application should send a single request at a time, and only send the next datagram once it has received a reply. If the reply takes too long to arrive, the application should either give up or try sending the same datagram again.

Datagrams are also suitable to transmit data flows in which occasional data loss is acceptable, such as when transmitting a live telephone call, where small audio glitches don't matter much.

Transmission Control Protocol

The transport layer can do more than match data from IP packets with their corresponding application sockets. When using the Transmission Control Protocol (**TCP**) instead of UDP, hosts will add *even more* extra information to IP packet payloads. This allows TCP to offer functionalities that enhance the reliability of communications between applications.

When using TCP, applications exchange data as if a direct communication line with the other application existed—even though IP packets have a limited size and routers cannot be trusted to deliver them. Behind the scenes, hosts split data in shorter chunks and deal with lost, duplicate, and disordered packets. The application must simply ask its host to create a connection with another application and then request for its data to be sent or received.

You can imagine UDP sockets as mailboxes that send and receive short, one-off messages to and from other boxes, with no guarantee of delivery. TCP sockets are different. Picture an active TCP socket as one end of a virtual pipe to another socket. All data sent through a TCP socket can be trusted to arrive intact. Let's see how to build this on top of the unreliable IP packet delivery system.

TCP Segments

With TCP, application data is split and communicated through payloads called **segments**. Similarly to UDP datagrams, TCP segments bundle the data with some extra information:

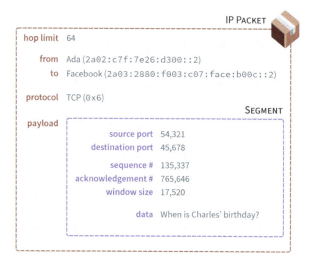

Figure 1.30 A simplified representation of a segment. Packets carrying segments have their protocol number set to 0x6.

Each of these fields is necessary for TCP to guarantee the integrity of the full, reassembled data:

PORT NUMBERS A host typically manages multiple TCP channels for its different applications. Once a segment arrives, there must be a way for a host to match it with the communication channel to which it belongs. To this end, segments carry their source and destination port numbers. A TCP channel of communication can be uniquely identified by four numbers: the IP addresses of the hosts, and two port numbers—one chosen by each host.

SEQUENCE NUMBER The sending host splits the application data in a sequence of small chunks. It assigns a **sequence number** to each chunk to indicate how they should be ordered. Each chunk is fit in a segment with its respective sequence number, and the segments are transmitted one-by-one on board individual IP packets. If segments arrive out of order, the receiving host reorders them using their sequence numbers. If a segment arrives twice, the host will notice the repeated sequence number and discard the duplicate data.

ACKNOWLEDGMENT NUMBER Communication is bidirectional with TCP: remote applications must *simultaneously* exchange segments. In order to keep track of which segment each host has received, they each include an **acknowledgment number**. It corresponds to the sequence number of the next segment the host expects to receive from its counterpart. For example, if Charles sends a segment with the acknowledgment number **44** to Ada, he acknowledges that he received all her segments until the sequence number **43**. If he has no data to send her, he must still send segments without data for acknowledgment purposes:

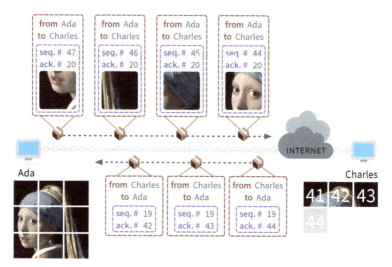

Figure 1.31 Charles receives an image from Ada. He has no data for her, so he sends empty acknowledgment segments. Notice that the sequence numbers of his segments don't increase. While sending her data, Ada signals she is ready to receive Charles' segment № 20.

After sending a non-empty segment, the sending host starts a timer for the receipt of its acknowledgment. If an acknowledgment takes too long to arrive, the sender assumes the packet was lost, retransmits the unacknowledged segment, and resets the timer.

Hosts monitor the time it takes for acknowledgments to arrive. When the time increases, it's a sign that the network is getting congested, so hosts reduce the rate at which they send out segments. When acknowledgment times decrease, it's a sign that more bandwidth is available, so hosts send segments at a higher rate. This is called **congestion control**, and it ensures network bandwidth is appropriately utilized.

WINDOW SIZE If a host receives too many segments at once, its computational resources can get overwhelmed. To ensure they are always capable of processing incoming data, hosts include a **window size** alongside the acknowledgment number. It indicates the number of bytes of data they are willing to receive beyond the last segment they acknowledged.

Senders suspend their transmission of unacknowledged segments whenever their total size reaches the window size of their counterpart. This is called **flow control**, and it ensures the computational capabilities of each host isn't exceeded. Using TCP, applications don't have to worry about congestion control and flow control, as those are taken care of by their hosts. On the other hand, applications using UDP are responsible for adapting the sending rate to the network bandwidth and to the computational resources of their counterparts.

TCP CHECKSUM Similarly to UDP datagrams, TCP segments include a checksum. It is added by the sending host and verified by the receiving host. If a corrupted segment is received, it is discarded without being acknowledged. This ensures all chunks of data eventually reach their destination free of errors.

TCP Connection

TCP communications are always conducted through a pair of segment threads called a **TCP connection**, as seen on Figure 1.31. Before two applications can start exchanging data through a TCP connection, their hosts must be able to recognize and sort the segments of that connection. They do so by remembering which port numbers correspond to which thread. Each host also chooses an initial sequence number to start its side of the connection, and it acknowledges the initial sequence number of its counterpart.

For these reasons, establishing a TCP connection requires the exchange of three segments between the client and the server. The first two segments carry a special SYN flag[16] that serves to **syn**chronize the sequence and acknowledgment numbers of the threads. Additionally, an ACK flag is carried by segments whose **ack**nowledgment numbers are valid and synchronized. The third segment can already begin carrying application data:

---

[16]Fields that are encoded by a one or zero are called **flags**.

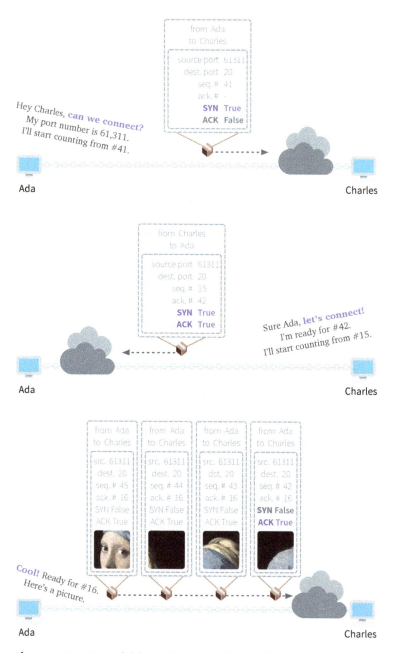

Figure 1.32 Hosts initiate TCP connections with random sequence numbers. We consider the connection is fully established from the moment the third segment is received, as both hosts obtained an acknowledgment of their sequence number.

Before the segment exchange in Figure 1.32 takes place, Charles has to ask his host to expect incoming TCP connection requests at port number 20. When Ada requests her host to start a new connection with Charles on port 20, Ada's host picks a port number at random to assign the connection—here, the port 61,311 was chosen.

As long as a connection is active, hosts keep track of sequence numbers, acknowledgment numbers, and window sizes. They time acknowledgments from their counterparts and decide when to send the next segments accordingly. The application remains blissfully unaware of all this work, as it simply calls TCP socket methods to connect, send, and receive.

TCP Sockets

TCP sockets are either active or passive. Only active sockets can be bound to a connection. When TCP sockets are created, they're active by default. Here's how a client starts a connection:

```
active_socket ← Socket.new(IP, TCP)
port_number ← 80
server_ip ← 2a03:2880:f003:c07:face:b00c::2
active_socket.connect(server_ip, port_number)
active_socket.send("When is Charles' birthday?")
```

The client must simply indicate the IP address of the server-host and the port number the server is listening to. All the procedures to start and maintain the TCP connection are performed by the host behind the scenes. After connect() ran successfully, send() and recv() can be called to exchange data.

In order to expect and accept connection requests at a given port number, a passive socket must be used. A socket is made passive after it is bound to a port number and its listen() method is called. Here is how a server waits for a connection on port 80:

```
server_socket ← Socket.new(IP, TCP)
server_socket.bind(80)
server_socket.listen()
active_socket ← server_socket.accept()
```

The server selects its port number. If another application already has a socket bound to the same port, bind() throws an error.

When accept() is called, the server halts until a new connection request comes in, at which point a new TCP connection is created. The new connection is bound to a freshly created active socket. The original passive socket can be used to accept more connections to other hosts. The newly created active socket can be used to communicate with the client by calling send() and recv() on it.

Often, servers will keep running accept() in a loop to establish many TCP connections with multiple clients and communicate with all of them simultaneously. That's how a web server is able to serve thousands, or even millions of different client applications at the same time.

This was a very simplified overview of how TCP connections work. There are numerous edge cases we haven't discussed. Segments carry extra flags to indicate urgency, error states, network congestion, connection termination, and more. Although TCP was originally designed shortly after IP in 1974, its inner workings are still changing to this day—for example to improve congestion handling and to optimize bandwidth usage.

If you're not specialized in networking, TCP sockets allows you to remain blissfully unaware of all these details. They are an example of sound systems engineering: they provide a simple interface to carry out complicated operations with little required knowledge of the underlying intricacies.

Conclusion

The Internet is one of mankind's greatest technological achievements, and it is the result of a tremendous amount of engineering and international cooperation. Computer programs virtually anywhere in the world can faultlessly and effortlessly communicate with each other, without the need for central coordination.

Such communications utilize physical and virtual connections at different levels of hardware and software. When applications communicate, it is therefore natural for their data to be encapsulated in several layers of packaging:

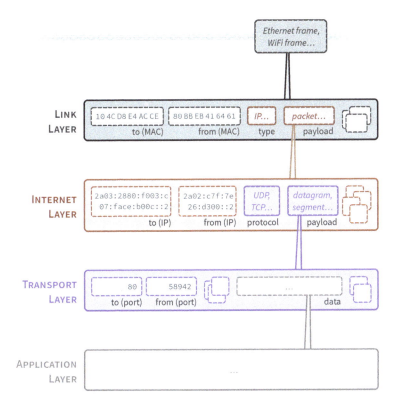

LINK LAYER Antennas, cables, and other equipment for manipulating electromagnetic waves allow pairs of computers to beam signals to each other. Link layer protocols allow these pairs of computers to harness these signals in order to exchange data in frames. Among other things, each frame contains the MAC addresses of its sender and recipient, a payload, and a field indicating the rules for handling the payload in the internet layer.

INTERNET LAYER Special computers called routers can connect different networks into larger networks, such as the Internet. Thanks to the Internet Protocol, payloads packaged as IP packets can hop from one frame to the next and thus travel between computers that don't share a direct physical link. Among other things, each packet contains the IP addresses of its origin and final recipient, a payload, and a field indicating the rules for handling that payload in the transport layer.

TRANSPORT LAYER Distant computers host applications that wish to communicate. Thanks to protocols such as UDP and TCP, multiple payloads expressed as datagrams or segments can form streams of data between distant applications. Among other things, each datagram or segment contains a chunk of application data along with the source and destination ports through which that data is flowing.

Both TCP and UDP are used in different ways depending on the nature of the communications between applications. In the next chapter, we will cover the **APPLICATION LAYER:** how we harness IP, TCP, and UDP to build the many modern Internet services we use every day, such as email and the World Wide Web.

This layered architecture for networking has been around for a while. In 1975, IP packets carrying TCP payloads were already traveling internationally between computers in Stanford and London. Protocols evolve—IP received an upgrade in 2012, and TCP has been tweaked many times—but the fundamental mechanics of the Internet have not changed for decades.

In this chapter, we covered essential networking concepts that will likely keep us connected for many more years. Let's now learn how we can harness Internet connectivity to power digital services such as electronic mail and the World Wide Web.

Reference

- Warriors of the Net
  - Watch it at http://code.energy/net-warriors
- Introduction to Networking, by Charles Severance
  - Get it at http://code.energy/severance

CHAPTER 2

Communication

> The Internet works because
> a lot of people cooperate
> to do things together.
> —JON POSTEL

OUR VOICE ENABLES us to send sounds to others, but this isn't enough to communicate. For two people to exchange thoughts through speech, they must share a common language. Likewise, transport protocols enable data to flow between applications, but it isn't enough for applications to understand each other and work together. In addition to connections, applications need communication rules.

Many communication rules that emerged during the early days of the Internet are still widely used by applications today. If you want your applications to participate in the Internet, you need to get acquainted with some of them. In this chapter, you'll learn to:

- Assign **names** to online addresses,
- Synchronize clocks to universal **time**,
- **Access** and use distant computers,
- Send and receive **mail** electronically,
- Browse the **Web** of documents and services.

Each independent set of communication rules forms a protocol, and the collection of all such protocols constitutes the **application layer**. The first application layer protocol we'll see works like an address book, which is directly or indirectly consulted by nearly every application that connects to the Internet.

2.1 Names

We can only send an IP packet to a host if we know its IP address. Yet, we never even memorize IP addresses of mainstream hosts such as Google's, Amazon's, or Facebook's.

Engineers realized it's impractical to refer to hosts using big numbers, so they created the **D**omain **N**ame **S**ystem, or **DNS**: a way to associate easy to read names with IP addresses. Thanks to DNS, we can contact hosts using names like `google.com`, `amazon.com`, or `facebook.com`.

When you type `facebook.com` in a web browser, it uses DNS to find an IP address linked to that name. It can then request the website by sending IP packets to that address. If you had directly typed Facebook's IP address in the browser, the DNS registry wouldn't have been consulted; yet the same web page would still show.[1]

DNS depends on the cooperation of many computers across the Internet. These computers communicate according to the DNS protocol to maintain the name registry. Most Internet applications, such as web browsers and email clients, use DNS to find the IP addresses of the hosts they have to connect with. But before we can explore the rules of this protocol, let's learn some underpinning concepts—starting with the hierarchical structure of the names.

Domains

Names in DNS are called **domain names**, or **domains**. They're made of text labels separated by dots. Labels can use the 26 letters from **a** to **z**, digits from **0** to **9**, and the hyphen (**-**). For example, `book-2.code.energy` is a domain with three labels.

Dots indicate hierarchical subdomains. Subdomains are domains overseen by a shorter parent domain: `book-2.code.energy` is a subdomain of `code.energy`. Likewise, `code.energy` is a subdomain of the single-label domain `energy`. Note that domains are case-insensitive: `code.energy` and `coDE.enERgy` are the same.

Every domain has an owner. Owners can create subdomains of their own domains. Ownership of a subdomain is transferable at

---

[1] See for yourself, visit the website http://[2a03:2880:f003:c07:face:b00c::2].

anytime by the parent domain owner. For example, Verisign is an American company that owns both com and net. In 1997, at the request of a small team of nerds, Verisign created google.com and granted them ownership over it.

Single-label domains, such as com, net, and energy, are called Top Level Domains, or TLDs. Due to the way it was designed, DNS is more efficient when there's a limited number of TLDs. For this reason, creating new TLDs is difficult by design. Usually, when individuals and organizations want a domain, they request a subdomain from the owner of an existing TLD, most notably com.[2]

Nonetheless, many powerful organizations possess their own TLDs. In 2014, Google was granted the google TLD.[3] In 2016, Motorola was granted the moto TLD. More critically, Amazon is trying to obtain the amazon TLD, but the governments of Brazil and Peru oppose the venture as they consider the name belongs first and foremost to their rainforest.

ICANN

In order for domain names to be universally understood, there must be a way for everyone to agree on who has ownership of each TLD. This requires consensual processes for the creation of TLDs and for the resolution of conflicts over their ownership. To this end, it was decided that an American non-profit organization, the Internet Corporation for Assigned Names and Numbers (ICANN),[4] has ultimate authority over TLDs.

When ICANN authorizes the creation of a TLD, it often requires the new owner to allow the general public to register subdomains. That is the case for most of the existing TLDs, including com, net, and energy. In order for Verisign to maintain their ownership of com, they are required by ICANN to accept requests for the creation of .com subdomains by anyone.

Sometimes, ICANN allows owners of TLDs to use them for exclusive interests. For instance, gov and mil are controlled by the

---

[2]You can find the list of TLDs at http://code.energy/tlds.
[3]Visit the website http://about.google to see for yourself.
[4]ICANN controls IANA, the organization that allocates IP address prefixes.

US government. They only create domains for American government bodies, such as **nasa.gov** and **spaceforce.mil**. Likewise, the owner of **edu** only allows American educational institutions to have .edu domains, such as **mit.edu** and **caltech.edu**; and Google uses their TLD exclusively for company affairs, such as **grow.google** and **blog.google**.

In addition to general-use TLDs and exclusive-use TLDs, ICANN assigns two-letter country-code **TLD**s and cedes their control to their respective governments. Colombia has **co**, the United States has **us**, and the British Indian Ocean Territory has **io**.[5] Occasionally, ICANN creates TLDs for famous geographical areas. For instance, **rio** was given to the Rio de Janeiro city council.

Name Servers

DNS records link data to domains. A domain can have many records, each binding a chunk of data to the domain. All records have a code that indicates the type of information they carry. For example, **AAAA** records link a domain to an IP address:[6]

```
sprint.net.     AAAA  2600::
```

All DNS records must be stored on **name servers**: special hosts that will share their records with anyone on the Internet at any time. A domain's owner must grant at least two name servers with the authority to store its DNS records. Domain owners may either provide these servers themselves or hire third parties to do so.

Ownership of domains is enacted through DNS records. For example, recall Verisign owns **com**. In principle, Verisign's name servers would contain all records for .com domains, including **google.com**. However, this is not the case, because Verisign keeps the following records in its name servers:

---

[5]The TLDs are assigned following ISO 3166-1 alpha-2 country codes, with a few exceptions such as the United Kingdom. Their country code is GB but they were given the uk domain.

[6]Notice the **sprint.net.** domain. In official records, all domains end with a dot. In everyday use, the final dot is most often omitted for convenience.

```
google.com.        NS   ns1.google.com.
google.com.        NS   ns2.google.com.
ns1.google.com.  AAAA   2001:4860:4802:32::a
ns2.google.com.  AAAA   2001:4860:4802:34::a
```

An **NS** record states that the given **N**ame **S**erver has authority over a domain. With the above records, Verisign delegates the responsibility to store all records associated with `google.com`. In effect, it hands control of the domain to Google, who hosts the cited name servers. This gives Google the authority to set DNS records for `google.com` in their own name servers.

ROOT SERVERS Some special name servers, called **root servers**, are appointed by ICANN to have the authority to store DNS records of TLDs. New TLDs are created when ICANN asks **NS** records to be added to these servers. There are 13 root servers—ICANN makes their IP addresses well known. The University of Maryland, NASA, and the US Army are some of the entities that host a root server.

Querying

Name servers have two functions: store records and answer queries. Most Internet applications rely on them. Your web browser, for example, only works if it has a way to discover the IP addresses of the websites you wish to reach.

Name servers expect queries on UDP port 53. Typically, a DNS query message and its reply fit in one datagram. To illustrate how it works, let's query name servers using the `dig`[7] program. It sends a datagram to the IP address we specify, containing a query that conforms to the DNS protocol. `Dig` is invoked from the command line as follows:

```
dig @[address] [domain] [type]
```

---

[7]The `dig` program comes pre-installed on Linux and MacOS terminal emulators. If you don't have access to a command-line interface, use http://code.energy/dig. If you don't know what the command line is, don't worry! We will learn more about it later in this chapter.

This sends a datagram to the given address on UDP port 53, asking for records of a specific type, associated with the given domain. When a datagram arrives in response, dig decodes it and displays the records in plain text.

Suppose we want to connect with icmc.usp.br, but we only know the IP address of NASA's root server: 2001:500:a8::e. Let's ask NASA what's the name server responsible for icmc.usp.br:

```
dig @2001:500:a8::e icmc.usp.br. NS
```

The root server replies with the following records:

```
br.                    NS   a.dns.br.
a.dns.br.              AAAA  2001:12f8:6::10
```

We can immediately see that NASA doesn't have the **NS** records for icmc.usp.br. In fact, root servers shouldn't even be expected to store these records: **br** is a country-code TLD under the authority of the Brazilian government. The root server helps us by indicating the IP address of the Brazilian server responsible for **br**. Let's take this advice and send our query there:

```
dig @2001:12f8:6::10 icmc.usp.br. NS
```

This time, we receive the specific records we asked for:

```
icmc.usp.br.           NS   c.dns.usp.br.
c.dns.usp.br.         AAAA  2001:12d0::8
```

We can now ask for the **AAAA** record associated with icmc.usp.br:

```
dig @2001:12d0::8 icmc.usp.br. AAAA
```

And at last, we receive the IP address we wanted:

```
icmc.usp.br.          AAAA  2001:12d0:2080::231:6
```

If our original query was a subdomain of icmc.usp.br, we may have needed to iterate our query for an **NS** record once more. This is called **iterative querying**, and it allows you to look up any DNS information starting with any single root server's IP address.

Recursive Querying

As of 2020, it's estimated that a few million DNS queries are made *every second*. If hosts only performed iterative querying, it would be extremely difficult for name servers to handle all those requests. Fortunately, most DNS queries are handled in a different way—one that minimizes the load on the name servers.

Some name servers, often called **DNS servers**, allow you to consult any DNS record through a single query. They are typically maintained by large organizations with a lot of throughput, such as Internet Service Providers. An ISP will almost always inform customer routers of its DNS server's IP address. Customer routers will often use that server for all their DNS queries.

Today, most home routers are capable of running their own DNS server. Typically, personal computers are configured to use their router as their default DNS server. If you invoke `dig` without an @ argument, your computer will probably query your router. In turn, your router will likely forward the query to the ISP's DNS server. Try it with the following command:

```
dig icmc.usp.br. AAAA
```

This is much faster: your DNS server is closer to you than any other name server. Furthermore, a single query gets you the DNS records you want. As the client, you don't even know (or care) whether your DNS server queried another DNS server or fetched the records directly from the name servers with authority over them.

We call this process **recursive querying**, because the client's single query propagates up a chain of DNS servers until the answer is found. Its advantage lies in **caching**: servers keeping past query results in their local storage, or *cache*. For instance, the first time a DNS server is queried about any `.io` domain, it asks a root server for `io`'s `NS` records; however, the next time a query for a `.io` domain is received, it retrieves the records from its cache instead of wasting the root server's time.

Since ICANN restricts the number of TLDs, it is easy for ISPs to cache all of them on their DNS servers, and therefore to only query the root servers sporadically. This design ensures that the root servers do not get overloaded.

On the flip side, caching slows down the propagation of changes around the network: DNS servers only update their cached NS records from time to time. Specifically, the Time To Live (**TTL**) value of a record indicates how long it may be stored in cache.

In previous examples, we've been omitting the TTL values for simplicity, but every record has one. It is typically displayed before the record type:

```
br.                    149836    NS   a.dns.br.
```

This record has a TTL value of 149,836, indicating that it may be cached for that many seconds. About 41 hours after this record is retrieved by a DNS server, it must be dropped from its cache. Setting a low TTL value makes future changes to the record propagate faster. However, higher TTL values allows servers to waste less resources on refreshing cache.

Types of Records

We've seen two DNS record types: **AAAA**, that links IP addresses to domains; and **NS**, that grants name servers authority over domains. Many other record types exist. Let's see the most common ones.

ADDRESS When DNS was invented in 1983, the **A** record type was used for IP addresses. In 2012, IP was upgraded and addresses became four times longer. The **AAAA** record type stores these new addresses for legacy IP to keep working unaffected as networks upgrade. Domains can have both records, for instance:

```
one.one.one.one.    AAAA   2606:4700:4700::1111
one.one.one.one.      A    1.1.1.1
```

If you have an outdated connection that only supports IPv4, you can query for **A** records and send IPv4 packets to the retrieved address instead of IPv6 packets.

TLDs can't have **A** or **AAAA** records. This is the reason why there is no website at http://com/ or http://google/. Single-label names are only used for addressing within Local Area Networks. The most common one is `localhost`, and it always points to a computer's own network interface.

MAIL EXCHANGE If you want to give Code Energy feedback on this book, you can write an email to hi@code.energy.[8] But how would your email system know where to dispatch your email for it to reach our servers?

Similarly to the Web, email depends on DNS. An **MX** record specifies a host responsible for receiving email for a domain. In order to send an email to maria@icmc.usp.br, the first step is to look up the **MX** records for `icmc.usp.br`. Let's dig:

```
dig icmc.usp.br. MX
```

Each **MX** record includes a host name and a priority number:

```
icmc.usp.br.          MX    1 aspmx.l.google.com.
icmc.usp.br.          MX    5 alt1.aspmx.l.google.com.
icmc.usp.br.          MX    5 alt2.aspmx.l.google.com.
icmc.usp.br.          MX   10 alt3.aspmx.l.google.com.
```

These records indicate that the owner of `icmc.usp.br` chose Google to receive email on their behalf. You can connect to any of those hosts to send an email to `icmc.usp.br`, but you should favor the one with the lowest priority number.

As for **A** and **AAAA** records, TLDs cannot have **MX** records. That's why there's no such email address as ada@io or larry@google.

CANONICAL NAME In the early days of the Web, people started to configure servers in their organizations for processing requests for web pages. It was usual to name such a server "www", so http://www.example.com/ became the expected web address for `example.com`. More recently, many are dropping the "www" part from their web addresses. A special **CNAME** record allow us to define a subdomain that's merely an alias:

```
www.code.energy.   CNAME   code.energy.
```

It instructs anyone trying to retrieve a record for `www.code.energy` to instead consider the records from `code.energy`.

---

[8]Do it!

TEXT It's possible to link arbitrary text to a domain using TXT records. This is often used for proving ownership of a domain, but you can use it for anything else. We left a special message for you in TXT records associated with **enigma.code.energy**. Will you be able to find the message? Remember, you can use **dig** to query any type of record that's linked to any domain.

Reverse DNS

DNS is most used to get an IP address from a given domain name. However, it also works in reverse: it can find which domain is associated with a given IP address. The trick is to re-express the IP address as a subdomain of ICANN's special TLD **arpa**. For example,

```
icmc.usp.br.                    AAAA    2001:12d0:2080::231:6
```

...becomes:

```
      ...d.2.1.1.0.0.2.ip6.arpa.    PTR   icmc.usp.br.
```
⎨‾‾‾‾‾‾‾‾‾‾‾‾‾‾‾‾‾⎬
  reversed IP address
  (32 hex digits)

Thanks to ICANN, there is a unique **arpa** subdomain corresponding to every IP address. A **PTR** record may be set for that subdomain in order to associate it with a domain name.

Authority over **arpa** belongs to IANA. When an IP address block is given to an organization, the organization also receives authority over the corresponding **arpa** subdomains. When a computer is allocated an IP address and a domain name, it's good practice to record the pair in a PTR record using the IP address's **arpa** subdomain.

With **dig**, you can query **PTR** records corresponding to any IP address using the -x argument. Try it:

```
dig -x 2600::
```

Reverse DNS is useful for confirming where an IP packet comes from. For instance, suppose you receive an IP packet carrying a message from **apple.com**. If the reverse DNS of the sender's IP address isn't an Apple domain, something is fishy!

That's because those who have the authority to set DNS records for `arpa` subdomains are careful. Most ISPs don't even allow their clients to set records on the `arpa` subdomains that correspond to their IP addresses.

Domain Registration

DNS doesn't just replace big numbers with names—it gives people the autonomy to reconfigure their networks. Think of a computer hosting a website. If it relocates, it receives a new IP address. The DNS records of the website can be updated to the new address such that visitors of the website won't notice the change!

This requires DNS to be universal. It must be easy, secure and affordable for anyone to own a domain. There are several rules that guarantee this. ICANN is liberal with exclusive-use TLDs: Google and IBM use `google` and `ibm` as they want. Also, ICANN allows each national government to set the rules for its country-code TLD. However, ICANN imposes strict rules on general-use TLDs meant for the public, such as `com, org, rocks` and `energy`.

ICANN calls an entity that has control of one or more TLDs a **registry**, or a Network Information Center (**NIC**). As we've seen, the registry for `com` is Verisign. ICANN makes it mandatory for general-use TLD registries to accept domain registrations by anyone. ICANN also stipulates that a registry cannot directly receive any domain registration applications.

In an effort to bolster competition and maximize the reach of DNS, ICANN stipulates that domain registration applications for general-use TLDs must be processed by companies called **registrars**. As of 2020, the largest registrar is GoDaddy: it has processed dozens of millions of domain registrations.

Registrars must be approved by ICANN. ICANN sets the maximum and minimum fees that registries and registrars may charge for a domain registration. Each time a domain is registered, part of the fee is paid to ICANN.[9] Technically, the domain is still owned by ICANN and is leased for a maximum of 10 years. However, since the lease is renewable, we generally refer to the lessee as the owner.

---

[9]As of 2020, ICANN charges $0.18 per year and per domain.

WHOIS Originally, ICANN obliged registrars to disclose the name and contact information of domain owners in a public directory called **WHOIS**. This directory functions through a different Internet protocol, independent of DNS. The directory can be consulted using the `whois` program on the command line:[10]

```
whois code.energy
```

Thanks to the advance of data protection norms and regulations, ICANN now allows registrars to redact the identity of domain owners. In 2012, ICANN has vowed to "reinvent **WHOIS**"; but as of 2020, the process is still ongoing.

DNS Hosting In theory, when registering a domain, you should provide the names and IP addresses of your name servers. This information is forwarded from your registrar to the registry for inclusion in the TLD name servers. However, most people don't even know what a name server is. To make things easier, many registrars offer a DNS hosting service: they use their own name servers on your behalf, and allow you to manage your DNS records through a web interface.

Names Market We live in the times of a booming online economy. Domain names are seen as virtual real estate and are sometimes sold for millions. For example, in 2019, GoDaddy brokered the sale of `voice.com` for $30 million. The `.com` domain names are so valuable that all possible four-letter combinations are taken.

Now that you know how DNS works, we will refer to hosts using their domain names. Whenever you see a domain name used as the address of a host, remember that a DNS query is necessary to find the IP address and send the IP packet.

---

[10]If you don't have access to a command-line interface, consult WHOIS here: http://code.energy/whois.

2.2 Time

Thousands of years ago, humans started figuring out how astronomy and mechanics could help quantify time. Ancient civilizations developed different lunar and solar calendars to track seasons and invented devices such as sundials and water clocks to track time within the day or night.[11]

As Roman legions professionalized in the 1st century BC, they increasingly kept time in order to harness their full military potential. Timekeeping allowed them to *coordinate* precise maneuvers and deliver devastating blows to their enemies. They also systematically recorded the time at which intelligence was collected by scouts and messengers so they could *correlate* events and gain insights into enemy tactics.

Today, we rely heavily on timekeeping as trucks, trains, ships and planes must *coordinate* to carry unfathomable amounts of goods around the world. We keep logs, sometimes every time a postal package changes hands. If everyone agrees on what time it is, we can *correlate* events so incidents and their consequences can be monitored, and people can be held accountable if they do something wrong.

In a similar way, timekeeping allows interconnected computers to form powerful teams. If distant computers can agree on what time it is, they can *coordinate* their actions at speeds that humans can't achieve. For example, financial transactions between parties on different continents can be confirmed within seconds.

Computers also store logs of each of their actions with a record of the exact time it occurred, called a **timestamp**. Agreeing on time allows interconnected computers to chronologically order past actions, records, and messages and therefore to *correlate* events. This mostly helps programmers find bugs, but can also, for example, help security specialists detect and track malicious activity.

Sharing time allows coordination and event correlation on epic scales. This begs the question: how do interconnected humans and computers even agree on what time it is?

---

[11] Sundials indicate the time when they're exposed to sunlight by casting a shadow on a marked surface. Water clocks track elapsed time from the gradual flow of water from one container to another.

Coordinated Universal Time

During the Age of Exploration, European sailors perfected their navigation techniques based on celestial observations and timekeeping. By the 18th century, they could precisely pinpoint their location at sea by using tables published by the Royal Greenwich Observatory in London. This worked as long as they knew exactly what time it was according to the observatory, so ships kept mechanical clocks[12] synchronized with Greenwich. As these reliable sources of time sailed around the world, Greenwich time gradually became the universal time standard.

A couple of centuries later, we switched from mechanical clocks to quartz clocks and atomic clocks[13] for more precision. Today, hundreds of atomic clocks track universal time. The Coordinated Universal Time, or **UTC**,[14] is the average of the measurements from these clocks, and it's currently our best standard for time. Thanks to advances in astronomy and planetary sciences, we can even account for Earth's slowing rotation: we occasionally add leap seconds to UTC so it stays synchronized with solar time in London.

All around the world, official time is obtained by adding an offset to UTC. The offset can change seasonally. For instance, the UK is an hour ahead of UTC half the year because of daylight saving time. Tokyo is nine hours ahead of UTC, year-round.

TIMEZONES Regions where the official time follows the same UTC offset form a **timezone**. IANA keeps track of the ever-changing timezones and their offsets and publishes them in the **tz database**. For instance, a big chunk of the eastern United States, from Miami to New York, shares the same UTC offset. In the tz database, this timezone has the code `America/New_York`. Britain is entirely in the `Europe/London` timezone, and Japan is in `Asia/Tokyo`.

---

[12]Mechanical clocks typically store energy with a weight or spring, and have a clever mechanism that lets the energy escape at constant time intervals.

[13]Quartz clocks use clever electronics and a special crystal to create vibrations at a precise and predetermined frequency. Atomic clocks are similar to quartz clocks, but they continuously sync the vibrations to atomic physics phenomena.

[14]English-speaking countries originally proposed the acronym *CUT*, while French speaking countries preferred *TUC*, for *temps universel coordonné*. The internationally recognized *UTC* is a compromise between the two.

Figure 2.1   Rough outline of the world's timezones as of 2020.

Computers track time in UTC, but typically display it according to their timezones. For example, an email sent to Tokyo from New York will carry a creation timestamp in UTC. This timestamp will be displayed differently for sender and receiver, according to the timezone configuration of their computers. Moving forward, when we refer to time, we mean UTC.

Network Time Protocol

Humans can aspire to British punctuality if their watches are correct down to the second. Computers however, work faster and their clocks need more precision. For example, a group of computers can log hundreds of records per second. In order to keep these records in chronological order, we must synchronize clocks down to the millisecond.

Adjusting clocks to such minute time scales is not an easy task. A naive approach would be to send a message on the Internet asking for the time from someone who knows it, and setting the clock to the timestamp received in response. However, this doesn't work: IP packets transit for undetermined durations. The time we received from a remote computer inevitably arrived late.

However, with some extra data, we can approximate how long a packet took to travel through the Internet. This duration can then be added to the indicated timestamp before we use it to adjust our clock. The **Network Time Protocol (NTP)** is the widely used standard for synchronizing clocks using this principle.

NTP timestamps are expressed in seconds since midnight on January 1st, 1900. For example, midnight on January 1st of the year 2000 has the timestamp 3,155,673,600. The number can have a fractional part, so it can capture time with very fine precision. NTP servers expect incoming messages at UDP port 123. An NTP message exchange works as follows:

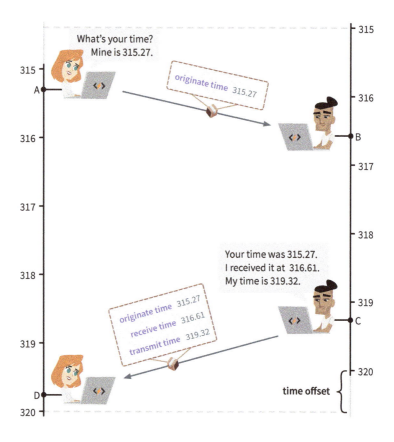

Figure 2.2 A client asks a server for the time using NTP. For simplicity, let's pretend we are in the year 1900, so that the timestamps are small numbers. The time kept by either computer runs from top to bottom.

The exchange starts when the client sends its time query. This message contains the time it was sent, according to the client's clock (time A). The server registers the time the message arrives, according to the server's clock (time B). When the server replies, it sends a message containing three times: time A, time B, and its response time (C). The client receives these times and confirms time A is the same it had previously sent. The client also notes when the reply arrives according to its own clock (time D).

On Figure 2.2, let's assume time D is 319.42. Knowing times A, B, C and D, the client can calculate the time the IP packets took to travel through the Internet:

$$\text{travel time} = \text{client roundtrip time} - \text{server processing time}$$
$$= D - A - (C - B)$$
$$= 319.42 - 315.27 - (319.32 - 316.61)$$
$$= 4.15 - 2.71$$
$$= 1.44.$$

It took 1.44 seconds for the messages to go from client to server and back. We estimate that it took half that time for the packet to travel from server to client: 0.72 seconds. The client should have received the reply 0.72 seconds after time C, at $319.32 + 0.72 = 320.04$. However, the client received the message when its clock was only at 319.42. This means the client's clock is running late compared to the server by about $320.04 - 319.42 = 0.62$ seconds.

NTP is conservative: it mandates clients adjust their clocks by only half the estimated offset. So our client pushes its clock 0.31 seconds forward. Every ten minutes, our client sends a new query and adjusts its clock accordingly. If packet travel times between client and server are identical in both directions, the client's clock will eventually synchronize with the server's clock. On typical Internet links, NTP synchronizes clocks with errors ranging in the tens of milliseconds.

Time Servers

You might be wondering where NTP servers obtain their time from. Most NTP servers actually synchronize to other NTP servers on the Internet: there's no problem running server and client NTP programs simultaneously.

However, this can lead to problems. Suppose Ada gets her time from Andrew, and Andrew gets his time from Charles, and Charles gets his time from Ada; none of the three will have a time source calibrated to UTC. Even if all of their clocks were initially correct, imprecisions would build up over time and cause them to drift away from universal time.

To prevent this problem, NTP servers are organized in a hierarchy called **clock strata**. A server that is directly linked to a reliable time source, such as an atomic clock or GPS receiver, is said to be *stratum 1*. Then, computers that synchronize with a stratum 1 server are said to be *stratum 2*. If a computer gets the time from a stratum 2 server, it becomes stratum 3, and so on. NTP rules that servers must report their stratum when answering time queries, and that the bottom-most level of the hierarchy is *stratum 15*.

This allows computers to avoid circular time-telling: if Charles is stratum 2, and tells the time to Andrew, Andrew becomes stratum 3. If Andrew tells it to Ada, she becomes stratum 4. If ever Ada tells Charles the time, he will know he must ignore it because he is stratum 2 and she is stratum 4. He must find a stratum 1 server to synchronize with.

There are many public NTP servers that answer queries from anyone. Apple computers are pre-configured to synchronize their clocks with time.apple.com, which is a stratum 2 server. Governments and large organizations often provide public NTP servers. For example, the United States government operates time.nist.gov, a stratum 1 public server.

NTP was created in 1985 and is one of the oldest protocols of the Internet. Since almost every computer runs an NTP client, people often take it for granted that their computers naturally know the time. You can check your clock at http://time.gov/. Odds are, it will be off by less than a second. Next, let's explore an Internet protocol that's even older than NTP.

2.3 Access

During the 19th century, human operators had to decode the electrical signals of the telegraph into language and vice versa. At the turn of the century, their job was made easier by a new device called the **teletype**. These machines were hooked to telegraph wires and incorporated a mechanical typewriter that could print incoming telegraphed characters automatically.

Teletypes also had a keyboard, so characters typed by their operator would be automatically telegraphed out through the wire. This allowed people to chat over long distances: messages typed into one machine would be printed by the second machine on the other side of the line.

Terminals

When electronic computers were first commercialized in the 1950s, they had no screens. In order to obtain feedback from their new machines, people had to link their input/output wires to teletypes. That way, they could feed data and instructions to the computer by typing, and their computer's response was printed back in real time. These teletypes that allow us to interface with computers through text are called **terminals**.

The computer program that processes information and instructions flowing to and from a terminal is called a **shell**. In order to communicate with humans, it operates a Command-Line Interface, or

CLI. As a terminal user types a command into the CLI, the shell acknowledges each character by asking the terminal to print it. In doing so, the user can always see what he or she is typing in real time. The user can input a **Non-Printing** Character (**NPC**) called the *carriage return*, and the shell executes the entire line as a command, optionally asks the terminal to print some output, and stands by for the next command.

In the 1960s, **glass teletypes** emerged. They worked exactly as older teletypes, except that they displayed characters on a screen rather than printing them on paper. That's why to this day, displaying text on a terminal screen is referred to as *printing*!

Screens allowed for the creation of the **cursor**: a movable indicator that specifies the location of interaction between the shell and the screen. Users started to use non-printing characters to ask the shell to move the cursor around. Crucially, cursors allowed previously printed text to be replaced or deleted, making interactions with computers more efficient. This sparked a surge in the development of computer programs with interactive text-based interfaces.

Video monitors were introduced in the late 1960s, and the first commercial computer with a Graphical User Interface (**GUI**) appeared in 1979. Today, virtually all personal computers such as laptops and phones run a shell that operates a GUI: we interact with icons and windows using mice, trackpads, and touchscreens.

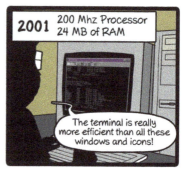
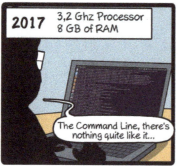
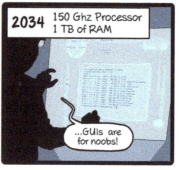

Figure 2.3 "Command Line", courtesy of http://commitstrip.com.

Still, many IT specialists continue to interact with computers via CLI. This can be by necessity—for example to operate GUI-less corporate servers—but also by preference. Many geeks use their GUI only to open a **terminal emulator**: an app that hooks into the CLI shell and transforms the screen and keyboard into a glass teletype.

Terminal emulators are powerful interfaces.[15] Via CLI, one can perform nearly any text-based task, such as organizing folders, sending emails, writing code and compiling software. We actually wrote and edited this book on terminal emulators!

```
ada@lovelylaptop:~$ dig babbage.code.energy. AAAA

; <<>> DiG 9.10.6 <<>> babbage.code.energy. AAAA
;; global options: +cmd
;; Got answer:
;; ->>HEADER<<- opcode: QUERY, status: NOERROR, id: 35327
;; flags: qr rd ra; QUERY: 1, ANSWER: 1, AUTHORITY: 0, ADDITIONAL: 1

;; OPT PSEUDOSECTION:
; EDNS: version: 0, flags:; udp: 1232
;; QUESTION SECTION:
;babbage.code.energy.            IN      AAAA

;; ANSWER SECTION:
babbage.code.energy.    516505  IN      AAAA    2620:0:862:ed1a::1

;; Query time: 24 msec
;; SERVER: 10.1.0.1#53(10.1.0.1)
;; WHEN: Wed Mar 03 09:53:40 CET 2021
;; MSG SIZE  rcvd: 76

ada@lovelylaptop:~$ _
```

Figure 2.4 Running `dig` on a Linux or MacOS terminal emulator.

Telnet

For most of the 1950s and 1960s, a terminal had to be wired directly to a computer in order to communicate with its shell. However, this changed in 1969, when engineers devised a way to connect terminals to any computer on a network. They called it **tel**etype **net**work, or **telnet**.

Terminal emulators can use telnet to access distant computer shells over the Internet. The CLI of a distant shell must be extremely reliable as unordered or missing characters could cause it to execute erroneous and potentially destructive commands. For this reason, the preferred transport layer protocol for telnet is TCP rather than UDP. Telnet servers typically expect connections on TCP port 21.

---

[15]Some passionate nerds showcased this by allowing you to watch Star Wars on a terminal: http://code.energy/terminal-movie.

When a TCP connection is established on port 21, the telnet server launches a shell and sends all incoming data from the connection into the shell. The output of the shell is sent to the client. On the client side, all characters typed by the user are transmitted to the server in real time, character by character. And when the client receives one or more characters, they're displayed on their terminal emulator.

Usually, after a telnet connection is established, the distant shell asks for a username and password for authentication. Once logged in, the telnet client works as a terminal hooked directly to the server. If a computer runs a telnet server, *any computer connected to the Internet can act as a terminal for that server.*[16] Geeks can operate a computer on another continent as if they were sitting right next to it with a screen and keyboard!

Communication protocols over the Internet are not exclusively used by geeks. Let's now have a look at the most popular applications of the Internet, starting with the best-known way of exchanging written messages.

2.4 Mail

In the 1960s, the few computers that existed were shared by many users. At that time, "mail" programs were already popular, but they only allowed a user to leave a message to a peer who worked on the same computer. These programs simply appended text to files that served as mailboxes. One mailbox file was attributed to each user. When users logged into their computers, alerts would appear if their mailboxes contained new messages.

During the 1970s, computer networks grew and the technology to access files in distant computers materialized. Mail programs evolved to append text to mailboxes of remote computers. This allowed users of distant computers to exchange messages as if they were on the same machine. Over time, programmers improved the

---

[16]Broad exposition to the Internet causes security risks and telnet is considered unsafe. Nowadays, we use a similar protocol called **Secure Shell** (**SSH**). The end user experience feels almost exactly like telnet, but it uses cryptography to deter hacking attacks. We explain it in the next chapter, so hang in there!

efficiency of these systems by gradually adopting a common message format, which looked like this:

```
From: White at SRI-ARC
Date: 24 JUL 1973 1527-PDT
Subject: Multi-Site Journal Meeting Announcement
NIC: 17996

At 10 AM Wednesday 25-JULY there will be a meeting
to discuss a Multi-Site Journal in the context of
the Utility.  Y'all be here.
```

The message starts with **headers**, which carry general information about the message, such as its sender, recipient, and subject. Each header takes one line, and a colon separates the header name from its value. After the headers, an empty line signals the start of the message body. These messages were widely used by computer geeks, who began calling them **email** (the **e** stands for electronic). To this day, the emails we exchange still follow this format!

In 1973, the above email could be replied to by appending a new message to the mailbox file `White` in the computer `SRI-ARC`. At the time, TCP/IP and DNS didn't exist, and computers were referred to by such nicknames. Later, the `at` was deprecated in favor of the @ symbol, so the mailbox in the example would be written `white@SRI-ARC`. For context, **SRI** stands for **S**tanford **R**esearch **I**nstitute, one of the organizations that helped to create and standardize this message format.

Mail Servers

Computers gradually became less expensive, and by the 1980s it wasn't uncommon for someone to be working on multiple machines. Yet, it would be easier to reach people by email on large scales if each person had a primary mailbox address at a single location. Many groups of users decided to monitor their primary mailbox on the same host, as if everyone still worked on a single computer. Organizations typically facilitated this by designating one of their computers as the **mail server**.

In those times, university students and tech engineers would have an account in their organization's mail server, regardless of which computers they happened to be using. Everyone's primary email address would point to this mail server. From their different computers, people would use telnet to log into the mail server and read emails stored in their individual mailbox files.

In 1985, DNS was rolled out, and it vastly improved the email system. Organizations started to adopt domain names and to create MX records to publicly announce their mail servers. Domain names became the standard addressing scheme for mailboxes. For instance, the mailbox named `White` in SRI's mail server would now be addressed as `white@sri.com`.

When given this email address, anyone could use DNS to discover the mail server that stores its mailbox file and send IP packets to that computer. However, in order to store a new message in someone else's server, one had to first be granted access to its mailbox files. This was cumbersome, so engineers started to invent ways for emails to be received without the external manipulation of any file on the receiving server.

This was the rise of email protocols. Just as NTP provides the framework for programs to exchange time, mail protocols allow programs to exchange emails. Various protocols were developed and soon every mail server abided by one of them. Emails could now be sent to virtually any location that IP packets could reach.

As any organization connected to the Internet could participate, email quickly gained prominence. What started off as simple notes left on a friend's desk was gradually becoming as important as traditional written correspondence.

In the 1990s, Internet Service Providers started bringing Internet access into people's homes. As one of their main selling points, ISPs often invited customers to open email accounts on their servers. In those years, personal computers were also starting to ship with email programs pre-installed. People mostly used them to connect to their ISP or employer's mail server.

And email spread like wildfire. Regular individuals flocked to the Internet in droves, sometimes solely in order to use email. One protocol stood out as the main enabler of this email revolution. Let's now learn how to transfer messages between hosts and email servers following that protocol.

Simple Mail Transfer Protocol

The most widely used email protocol is the Simple Mail Transfer Protocol (**SMTP**). It defines the conversation rules between an email server and a client computer. As we'll see, SMTP is more elaborate than *request–response* protocols[17] such as DNS and NTP.

First off, emails can contain messages that don't fit in a single IP packet. When an email is carried by many IP packets, it is important for their payloads to be pieced back together in order. For this reason, SMTP runs on TCP rather than UDP.

Mail servers expect incoming connections on TCP port 25. When a connection is established, the server starts the conversation. It sends a message to identify itself:

```
220 mail-server.example.com
```

All messages sent by the server start with a three-digit number, called the **return code**. SMTP defines many different codes, each with their own meaning. Specifically, `220` communicates that the server is ready to receive instructions. After the code, the server states its own name. In response, the client should send a `HELO` command to identify itself:

```
HELO client.code.energy
```

At this point, the server decides if it wants to continue the conversation, based on who the client claims to be. Some mail servers use reverse DNS and compare the client's self-reported name to the name that's linked to its IP address. If the mail server decides to continue, it will send a `250` response code, which means that the action requested by the client was accepted:

```
250 mail-server.example.com
```

With this exchange, both the client and the server acknowledged that they are about to transfer an email. They both also checked that they are communicating with their intended counterpart. Next,

---

[17]**Request–response** protocols are exactly what they sound like: a client sends a request to a server and then waits for a response.

the client is expected to give the return address of the email to be transmitted. If the server cannot deliver the client's email, it will send another email to the return address informing it of the issue:

```
MAIL FROM: <ada@code.energy>
```

Again, the server has the option to accept or reject this. Some mail servers are configured to only accept certain email addresses. If the address is accepted, the server returns the **250** code:

```
250 Ok
```

Next, the client must inform the server of the destination mailbox:

```
RCPT TO: <charles@example.com>
```

Again, the server confirms whether it accepts this destination mailbox. If the server accepts to receive the message, it will use the same **250** return code, informing the client that it can go ahead:

```
250 Ok
```

The client can now send the **DATA** command. This command asks the server to begin the transmission of the email message:

```
DATA
```

The server confirms and instructs the client to signal the end of the transmission with a line containing only a dot. The **354** return code informs the client that the server will consider the next characters it receives as part of the email message:[18]

```
354 End data with <CR><LF>.<CR><LF>
```

The client can then transmit the message. The **From**, **To** and **Date** headers are mandatory and must be present in every email. Other kinds of headers, such as **Subject**, are commonly used but are not required. The message body is also optional. Sending an email

---

[18]The non-printing characters <CR><LF> are a carriage return, followed by a line feed. This combination marks the end of a line.

without a body is similar to posting an empty envelope. Here's an example of an email the client could transmit:

```
From: <ada@code.energy>
Date: Wed, 27 Nov 2002 15:30:34 +0100
To: <charles@example.com>

That brain of mine is something more than
merely mortal; as time will show.
.
```

After the finishing `<CR><LF>.<CR><LF>` is delivered, the server checks that the received data is valid and formally accepts the message if that is the case. Many servers also inform the client of the internal ID that they assign to the received email:

```
250 Ok: queued as 1079212633C
```

At this point, the client can rest assured that the server will either deliver the message or **bounce**[19] it back with an error message. The client may continue by sending another `MAIL FROM` command to send more emails. Otherwise, it can politely say it's done by sending a `QUIT` command:

```
QUIT
```

Upon receiving this, the server should say goodbye and close the TCP connection:

```
221 Bye
```

A conversation similar to this one takes place every time you send an email—your email software performs it behind the scenes. Originally, there was no authentication in SMTP: servers blindly trusted clients were sending legitimate emails. Sadly, once email became popular, inconsiderate Internet actors started sending unsolicited junk to every email address they could find. The most malicious of them even send fraudulent emails with illegitimate `From` fields.

---

[19]SMTP was designed to be dependable, so mail servers won't drop an accepted email without notice. A rejected message is called a *bounce* because its content is returned to the sender.

Sending Emails

Email was initially created as an open system in which anyone could participate without asking any central authority for permission. Its pioneers hoped all participants would act in good faith. Unfortunately, as soon as email was widely adopted, this hope was lost. Nevertheless, engineers kept working to make email resilient to bad actors, without relinquishing its open nature.

At first, engineers started keeping public **blacklists**, which were frequently updated with names and IP addresses of known email abusers. Administrators configured their servers to automatically reject connections from blacklisted users. This mitigated the problem, but didn't fix it: abusers learned to use fresh IP addresses and domain names to send junk.

To this day, the majority of bad emails come from Internet connections provided by ISPs. Most organizations carefully police the use of their networks in order to protect their reputation. However, ISPs often service millions of users, and individually screening each one isn't viable.

Fortunately, it's easy to check whether an IP address belongs to a well established organization or to a home connection: you consult its reverse DNS record. ISPs don't allow residential clients to set these records, but all credible mail servers will have proper reverse DNS for their IP addresses. So mail servers have started restricting home IP addresses, which drastically reduces email abuse.

In order to implement this policy, SMTP has been upgraded to an extended version (**ESMTP**) with support for authentication via username and password. For all home users, `MAIL FROM` commands are only accepted after the user is authenticated through an `AUTH` command.

This is how sending an email works today: you compose an email, and your computer uses SMTP to submit it to your mail server. Your mail server then connects to the mail server associated with the destination mailbox and uses SMTP to relay your email. Since your mail server's IP address has a reverse DNS record, it can communicate to all other mail servers without authentication.

So email traffic is divided in two: users submitting messages to their own mail server and mail servers relaying messages to each other. Today, TCP port 587 is reserved for email submission, and port 25 is reserved for email relay. Home email users have stopped using TCP port 25.

Accordingly, most ISPs even drop home IP packets containing segments to port 25, effectively blocking home Internet users from performing email relay. Mail servers expect incoming connections on two TCP ports:

- Port 25, to receive emails from other mail servers,
- Port 465, to receive emails from authenticated users.

All this still isn't enough to curb the malicious email senders. The fight between engineers and senders of junk still rages on. In some cases, engineers guess which emails are junk using intricate sorting mechanisms. In others, they use cryptographic signatures to verify the sender email's address.

Retrieving Emails

At first, people read their emails by directly opening mailbox files. In most cases, people weren't sitting in front of their mail servers, so they would use telnet to open their mailbox files remotely. Engineers realized it would be easier if people could download their emails on their own computer and read them "locally". This would spare them the hassle of using telnet every time they needed to read an email.

Since SMTP wasn't a suitable way for a server to deliver email to an end user, another strategy was needed. After all, most users wouldn't have their computers online 24/7, ready to receive incoming SMTP connections. Therefore, new protocols were developed; they allowed users to initiate a connection to the mail server, get a list of emails in the mailbox, and select which ones to download from the list.

The most commonly used of such protocols is the Internet Message Access Protocol (**IMAP**). Its working principle is similar to SMTP, the server also conducts a conversation with the client using command codes and plain text. There are commands for clients to list the emails in their mailboxes and to request the transmission of a specific email.

Today, roughly half of the world's emails are sent and received through **webmail** services such as Gmail. These services offer the most hassle-free access to email, as they don't require you to install or configure a client application on your computer. Let's now explore the **Web**: the beautiful set of mechanisms that made this—and much more—possible.

2.5   Web

If a text document contains links referencing other documents, and these links allow you to jump back and forth across multiple documents, the text is said to be **hypertext**: the links create an extra dimension in the textual space. For example, *Wikipedia* is hypertext, but a physical encyclopedia is not. Hypertext doesn't have to be read linearly like regular text—it can be explored by navigating through the links.

As graphical user interfaces spread in the 1980s, knowledge workers discovered hypertext could make their jobs easier and more efficient. While early programs to read and write hypertext documents gained popularity, it was still impossible to create links between hypertext documents residing in different computers. Hypertext documents were largely isolated from each other.

With the advent of the Internet, a new hypertext system was created to overcome this limitation. Documents created and stored on different computers could finally be linked into a universal web of documents. The system was named the World Wide Web, or *WWW*—and its hypertext documents were named **web pages**. For it to work, different computers around the world had to share three basic components:

- A language to write web pages as files,
- A way to link web pages to each other,
- A protocol to transfer files between computers.

A program that uses these three components is a called a **web browser**. Virtually every web browser today agrees on a basic set of standards. Let's explore how they work.

Hypertext Markup Language

Web pages should be easy to create, while also being universally understandable by all Internet participants. To attain these goals, it was decided that web pages would consist of plain text, enriched with special tags for specifying structure and presentation.

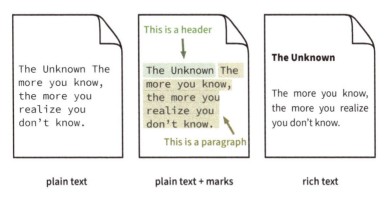

plain text   plain text + marks   rich text

Figure 2.5   Rich documents can be created by marking plain text.

Tags can be used to mark a paragraph, to set a phrase as a header, to emphasize a word, and much more. A collection of tags that can be mixed with text to extend it forms a **markup language**. Many different markup languages exist. The one created for the Web is called **H**yper**t**ext **M**arkup **L**anguage, or **HTML**. In HTML, any text that's enclosed by <...> characters is a tag. For example, this is how a header followed by a paragraph is expressed:

```
<h1>The Unknown</h1>
<p>The more you know, the more you realize you don't know.</p>
```

This example includes two HTML tag pairs: `<h1>...</h1>` and `<p>...</p>`. The `h1` tags indicate that "The Unknown" is a header. The `p` tags demarcate a paragraph. Many other tags exist besides these, and most are used to define the *structure* of the document.[20]

---

[20]Another language, called **C**ascading **S**tyle **S**heets (**CSS**), was later created to customize most aspects of how an HTML document and its structure are presented: fonts, layout, colors, etc.

Typically, HTML tags come as opening/closing pairs: each pair applies over a section of the document, and the closing tag includes a slash. However, a few tags, called **empty tags**, don't come in pairs. For instance, `<br>` is used to insert a line break in the text, and `<img>` is used to insert an image.

Complete HTML web pages must have two parts: the **head** and the **body**. The head contains information about the document which web browsers shouldn't display. The body, on the other hand, is meant to be displayed on screen by web browsers. Here is an example of a simple but complete HTML web page:

```html
<html>

    <head>
        <title>Daily quote</title>
    </head>

    <body>
        <h1>The Unknown</h1>
        <p>The more you know, the more you realize
        you don't know.</p>
    </body>

</html>
```

As you can see, the head and body are each wrapped in a tag pair with their respective name; and both are wrapped together in an `<html>` tag pair. Try creating a text file with this content, saving it as an `.html` file, and opening it on a web browser! Within an HTML file, spacing and line breaks are ignored by the browser. They're just used to make the file easier for humans to read.

Many tags can contain attributes that extend or complement it. For instance, the `<html>` tag can contain an attribute that specifies the document's language: `<html lang="en">`. Some tags have a mandatory attribute. For example, the `<img>` tag must specify which image to display:

```html
<img src="cat.gif">
```

The most important HTML tag is the anchor tag `<a>`. It transforms a section of the document into a link to another hypertext location. Consider the following example:

```
Everybody loves <a href="cats.html">them</a>.
```

Web browsers will render this line on screen as follows:

Everybody loves them.

Clicking the underlined word instantly switches to a different location as specified by the hypertext reference (`href`) attribute of the anchor. Let's now learn how to express these locations in order for web browsers to find them.

Uniform Resource Locator

The anchor's `href` parameter is a reference to a document that is shown once the anchor is clicked. It follows a simple format: two slashes, followed by the name of the host where the document lives, plus the path to the document. For example, here's a link to the document "/pets/cat.html", located in the `zoo.org` host:

```
<a href="//zoo.org/pets/cat.html">kitten</a>
```

Browsers interpret the document path as the location of a file within the host's file system. For instance, the document referenced by the anchor above is assumed to be a file named "cat.html" inside a "pets" directory.

RELATIVE REFERENCES If a reference doesn't start with any slashes, it is treated as a folder-relative reference. For instance, suppose this link exists in the //zoo.org/pets/cat.html document:

```
Are <a href="dog.html">they</a> our best friends?
```

Here, the `href` parameter refers to a file in the same directory as the present file (cat.html). Hence, the browser will interpret this reference as //zoo.org/pets/dog.html. There are also references with only one starting slash, which are host-relative:

```
<a href="/bugs/ant.html">Ants</a> are small.
```

This reference will be interpreted as //zoo.org/bugs/ant.html.

FRAGMENT REFERENCE There is a way to refer to a specific part, or fragment, of an HTML document. Suppose that the dog.html file looks like this:

```
<h1 id="bulldog">Bulldog</h1>
<p>…</p>

<h1 id="poodle">Poodle</h1>
<p>…</p>

<h1 id="golden">Golden Retriever</h1>
<p>…</p>
```

We can create an anchor that links directly to the header about the golden retrievers inside the dog.html document, like this:

```
<a href="dogs.html#golden">These dogs</a> rock!
```

The # character can also be used to jump to a different place *within* the document that is being accessed. For example, this trick is used in the *Contents* box of Wikipedia pages to allow you to jump directly to a section you're interested in.

Similar references are used when referring to other types of media resources, such as images. For instance, if there's a picture of a golden retriever on the `zoo.org` host, it can be included in the document like this:

```
<h1>Golden Retriever</h1>
<img src="/pics/golden-retriever.jpg">
<p>As you can see in this picture…</p>
```

SCHEME There's another important piece of information we can add to our web references: the *way* the resource will be accessed, known as the **scheme**. One that you might immediately recognize is `http`, the most widely used protocol to transfer web page files between computers. The scheme will appear in the beginning of a reference and is succeeded by a colon:

```
<a href="http://zoo.org/pets/cat.html">kitten</a>
```

A complete reference to a web resource—which includes a scheme, a host, and a document path—is called a Uniform Resource Locator, or **URL**. People also call them **web addresses**. Web browsers typically display the URL of the page they are rendering in a bar at the top. Let's now see how the `http` scheme works.

Hypertext Transfer Protocol

The most common action we perform when browsing the Web is to click a link to switch from the web page we are viewing to the next one. Every time a link is clicked, the web browser has to contact the computer hosting the referred document and retrieve a copy of that file. The **H**ypertext **T**ransfer **P**rotocol (**HTTP**) mediates these document transfers.

Since transferred documents can be larger than the MTU, HTTP relies on TCP rather than UDP. It has a client–server design: a web browser is the client application, and the web server expects connections on port 80. After a connection is established, the client sends a request. Once the server processes it, a response is sent back.

In 2015, HTTP received a major upgrade,[21] but the version from the 1990s is still widely used. Requests that follow the earlier version of HTTP are in plain text. The first line indicates the *request type*, the *document path*, and the *protocol version*. The next lines are used for headers, similarly to email messages. Finally, an empty line indicates the end of the request:

```
GET /pets/cat.html HTTP/1.0
User-Agent: Mozilla/5.0 (Macintosh)
Accept-Language: en-us
```

---

[21]The 2015 version of the protocol is referred to as HTTP/2. It adds several performance improvements over the previous version, but it doesn't change the general structure of the communicated information.

The above example shows the most common request type: GET. It indicates the client wants to retrieve a document. Headers are optional, but are almost always included. The example shows two of the most common headers. Accept-Language specifies that the English version of the document is preferred, and User-Agent says which web browser software and which computer operating system created the request. A typical response from a server to such a request looks like this:

```
HTTP/1.0 200 OK
Server: nginx/1.15.8
Date: Wed, 19 Aug 2020 20:46:53 GMT
Last-Modified: Sat, 20 Nov 2004 07:16:26 GMT
Content-Length: 49
Content-Type: text/html

<html><body><h1>Cats are cute!</h1></body></html>
```

The first line indicates the protocol version, followed by a three-digit status code, similar to the ones used in SMTP. Here, 200 means the request went through without any issue. Many more codes exist. For instance, 404 indicates that a requested document can't be found. Codes are grouped by their first digit. Namely, those starting with 2 signal successful requests, and those starting with 4 signal errors caused by inappropriate requests.

After the first line, optional headers are included. In our example, there are headers informing the client of the server's software, the date the message was sent, when the requested document was last changed, the type of document carried, and its total length. Many other headers are widely used for authentication, tracking, caching, and more.

HTTP has been incredibly successful, and it has grown to be used outside the World Wide Web. For instance, an app in your phone may send out an HTTP request to obtain raw weather data. The retrieved data can then be used to display weather conditions by a widget in the phone's interface, rather than on a web page provided by the server.

Web Apps

An HTTP request may carry a path referencing a program. In such cases, the server runs the program and responds with its output. For example, requests for /random at code.energy refer to a program that generates a page containing a random number. The server returns a **dynamic page**, rather than a static page that looks the same at every request. Visit this page on a browser and refresh it a few times to see for yourself:

```
http://code.energy/random
```

Dynamic pages can also receive inputs from the user as parameters. For instance, google.com has the dynamic page /search, which takes a parameter named q as a search query. The parameter is appended after the document path as follows:

```
http://google.com/search?q=energy
```

In order to load this web page, browsers can send this request:

```
GET /search?q=energy HTTP/1.0
```

Upon receiving this request, the web server calls the program associated to /search. Any parameter in the form ?name=value after the path is passed to the program. Input parameters in this form are called **query strings**.

Since there are characters that valid URLs cannot contain, there is a standard way of encoding them using the percent sign. For instance, the space[22] becomes %20 and ! becomes %2F. Query strings can include multiple parameters separated by ampersands (&). Visiting the following URL searches "code energy" and passes an additional num parameter for listing only five results:

```
http://google.com/search?q=code%20energy&num=5
```

Query strings are neatly integrated with HTML. Some tags, including <form> and <input>, can be added to web pages for a user

---

[22]In query strings, the space can either be encoded %20 or simply with a plus sign +. This does not work, however, elsewhere in the URL. Characters that have special functions (such as +, %, ?, =, and &) must also be encoded for those functions to be bypassed.

to easily enter and submit data using query strings. The following HTML code creates an input box to enter keywords and a button to dispatch the query:

```html
<form action="//google.com/search">
    <input name="q">
    <button>Search Google</button>
</form>
```

Once the button is pressed, an HTTP request of the GET type passes the text typed in the input to the server as a query string. On the server end, a program finds the links that it deems most useful for the user and sends them back within a web page document.

In general, programs that respond to HTTP requests of the GET type should perform no action other than to retrieve information. For example, a GET request shouldn't allow a user to post a status message on social media, delete a photo from a cloud drive, or place an order on an online shop. This means users can issue GET requests without worrying about consequences other than what will be shown on their web page.

In order to perform these other actions, there exist several other HTTP request types. For example, if the desired effect is to create something, the POST type should be used. An HTML form can be switched to send POST requests by setting a method parameter in the `<form>` tag:

```html
<form action="/send-message" method="POST">
    <p>Subject: <input name="subject"></p>
    <p>Message: <input name="message"></p>
    <button>Send message</button>
</form>
```

In POST requests, input data is carried in the body of the request rather than in the query string. However, the data is still encoded the same way. Here's a POST request that could be generated by submitting the form from the above example:

```
POST /send-message HTTP/1.0

subject=Greetings&message=Hello%20World%2B
```

It's possible to create intricate systems that can be operated from web browsers. A prime example are webmail systems such as Hotmail and Gmail. These websites allow people to use email through their browser. The web server is tasked with talking to mail servers, allowing users to send emails without directly establishing any SMTP connections from a web client.

To facilitate this, HTML pages can include JavaScript code. We can then program web pages with the same capabilities as other graphic applications! Increasingly, web pages are evolving from plain hypertext documents to full-fledged apps.

Conclusion

We learned about some of the most notable Internet applications and their protocols, but there are many more we haven't explored. For instance, we've seen in Chapter 1 that routers must regularly exchange connectivity information. To that end, they run applications that communicate using the **B**order **G**ateway **P**rotocol (**BGP**) on TCP port 179. If you want learn about BGP and other interesting protocols in depth, check the references at the end.

Port Numbers

We've seen how each protocol is associated to a specific TCP or UDP port number. Applications that use the same protocol almost always expect connections on the same port number. For example, you don't need to know which port number to use in order to retrieve a web page from a host—web servers expect connections on TCP port 80. IANA is the organization that decides which port number is standard for each protocol. When a new protocol is created, its developers send IANA an application to reserve a port number.[23]

Rather than developing a new protocol and applying for a port number, many application developers piggyback on existing

---

[23]Ports 0–49151 should only be used by protocols registered with IANA. Ports 49152–65535 are never assigned to any protocol and can be used for any purpose. You can check the current port number assignments at http://code.energy/ports.

generic protocols for communicating over the Internet. For example, many applications are made accessible over the Internet by integration with a web server. In such cases, HTTP is used to transfer raw data (rather than web pages) to and from the applications (rather than web browsers).

Peer-to-Peer

In this chapter, all the application layer protocols that we have explored follow a client–server architecture. However, there is an alternative architecture called **Peer-to-Peer** (**P2P**), where each application acts both as server and client. Notable examples of P2P protocols include BitTorrent, the file-sharing protocol, as well as Bitcoin and Ethereum, the two largest cryptocurrency networks.

Peer-to-Peer services eliminate intermediaries between users and have no central point of failure. BitTorrent, Bitcoin and Ethereum cannot be shut down. The United States military uses P2P technology extensively for troops to operate without central coordination and without relying on centralized infrastructure such as cellphone towers.

Security

One other important aspect of the Internet that we haven't addressed is its lack of security. Whoever is operating a router can read and modify data from any packet that reaches it. We've seen that IP packets are handled by many unknown routers as they move through the Internet. Therefore, we must consider all data traveling on board IP packets as potentially public information, and we can't completely trust that data received over the Internet hasn't been changed on the way. To mitigate this flaw, application layer protocols often include encryption schemes so the data can't be read or inconspicuously tampered with by intermediaries. In the next chapter, we'll see how it works.

Reference

- Computer Networking: A Top-Down Approach, by Kurose
  - Get it at http://code.energy/kurose
- Computer Networks, by Tanembaum
  - Get it at http://code.energy/tanenbaum

CHAPTER 3

Security

> Computer systems are not getting more secure.
> I hope that in the future, the advances we're
> making in cryptography are going to influence
> the fairly bad situation in cybersecurity.
>
> —ADI SHAMIR

P ROGRAMMERS ARE ENTRUSTED with the task of securing sensitive data, such as private messages, banking transactions, medical records, and more. It is your duty to protect this data from hackers. You must ensure that only those with valid credentials can access your systems and that confidential data cannot be read even if it is leaked.

The practice of securing data against attacks from unauthorized parties is called **cryptography**. An algorithm that reversibly encrypts data into an unintelligible form is called a **cipher**. Most systems can be secured using cryptographic libraries vetted by experts. In this chapter, we'll explore the underlying principles of ciphers and other tools cryptographic libraries provide. You'll learn to:

- 🗝️ Mess around with fun but insecure **legacy** ciphers,
- 🔑 Improve them to obtain strong **symmetric** ciphers,
- 🔐 Securely message strangers using **asymmetric** ciphers,
- #️⃣ **Hash** any amount of data into a digital fingerprint,
- 🖥️ Secure your networking **protocols** for a safer Internet,
- 🕵️ **Hack** your systems to find vulnerabilities before bad guys do.

If attackers successfully intercept encrypted data, there's a chance they will figure out how to unscramble the data and reveal its secrets. If that happens, we say the cipher used to encrypt the data was **broken**. Let's start by exploring ciphers that were popular in the past and which are easily broken today. This will help us understand why it's difficult to break modern ciphers.

3.1 Legacy

One of the earliest ciphers was used by Julius Cesar over two thousand years ago to send secret letters to his generals. His encrypted messages would look like this:[1]

```
GR QRW EULQJ DQB ERGB RI PHQ DFURVV WKH UKLQH
```

If a secret letter from Caesar was seized, the information contained in the letter would remain confidential. Caesar's enemies couldn't make sense of the encrypted messages, but his generals could easily read them. To encrypt messages, the Romans agreed in advance to shift every letter of the original message three positions forward in the alphabet, replacing the letters as follows:

```
A  B  C  D  E  F  G  H  I  J  K  L  M  N  O  P  Q  R  S  T  U  V  W  X  Y  Z
3  3  3  3  3  3  3  3  3  3  3  3  3  3  3  3  3  3  3  3  3  3  3  3  3  3
↓  ↓  ↓  ↓  ↓  ↓  ↓  ↓  ↓  ↓  ↓  ↓  ↓  ↓  ↓  ↓  ↓  ↓  ↓  ↓  ↓  ↓  ↓  ↓  ↓  ↓
D  E  F  G  H  I  J  K  L  M  N  O  P  Q  R  S  T  U  V  W  X  Y  Z  A  B  C
```

Messages were then decrypted by shifting the letters back. This is known as the **shift cipher**. Since Caesar's enemies never discovered how it worked, it provided enough security. However, anyone who knows about this cipher can easily break it, even if letters are shifted more than three positions: there are only 25 possible shifts for the Latin alphabet. An attacker can break the cipher by trying them one by one until the message makes sense.

Let's have a look at a few useful terms. An encrypted message is called a **ciphertext**. To decrypt a ciphertext, we need to know which cipher was used, and which **encryption key** was used with it. For the shift cipher, the key is the number of positions in the alphabet that letters are shifted. Knowing cipher and key, we can undo the encryption and recover the original data, called the **plaintext**.

---

[1]In reality, messages would look slightly different because Caesar only knew 23 letters... and didn't speak English.

SECRET CODE 🫤 Flipping through the pages of an old book from your grandmother's library, you come across this handwritten footnote:

```
MAXI KBVX HYLX VNKB MRBL XMXK GTEO BZBE TGVX
VTKX EXLL VHFF NGBV TMBH GLVH LMEB OXL
```

She tells you she used to have fun with the shift cipher when she was a teenager but can't remember what the cryptic writing means. Can you recover the plaintext?

The simplest way to crack a shift cipher is to test different keys on the ciphertext and see if the output makes sense. There are only 25 possibilities! You can find the solution in Appendix II.

Zigzag Cipher

There's a way to scramble the plaintext which does not require any letter substitutions. Instead, the letters are shuffled in a pre-arranged way. For example, consider the following dispatch:

```
We were found. Flee at once.
```

Let's first remove all unnecessary formatting, as it could give out clues about the cipher. Typically, all letters are capitalized, punctuation is omitted and spaces are either removed or replaced by Xs:

```
WEXWEREXFOUNDXFLEEXATXONCE
```

We now write each letter on a different line than the previous. For example, let's follow a zigzag pattern across three lines:

The final ciphertext is obtained by joining the three lines together:

```
WEFDETC
EWRXONXLEAXNE    →    WEFDETCEWRXONXLEAXNEXEUFXO
XEUFXO
```

This is called the **zigzag cipher**, and its encryption key is the number of lines used by the pattern. This cipher suffers from the same fragility as the shift cipher: only a limited number of keys are possible. One can easily break the cipher by testing the reverse process for every possible number of lines.

Substitution Cipher

Let's go back to ciphers that replace letters in the plaintext. A cipher that has a different rule for replacing each letter is more secure than the shift cipher. For instance, you could meet a friend and agree on the following map of letter substitutions.

```
A  B  C  D  E  F  G  H  I  J  K  L  M  N  O  P  Q  R  S  T  U  V  W  X  Y  Z
↓  ↓  ↓  ↓  ↓  ↓  ↓  ↓  ↓  ↓  ↓  ↓  ↓  ↓  ↓  ↓  ↓  ↓  ↓  ↓  ↓  ↓  ↓  ↓  ↓  ↓
V  H  I  E  R  P  X  N  D  J  F  T  G  L  B  W  O  Q  K  Z  M  U  C  S  Y  A
```

This is a **simple substitution cipher**. Here, ENERGY would be encrypted RLRQXY. The encryption key is the above map specifying how letters are replaced. There are 26! ways to shuffle the alphabet and create different keys.[2] This means there are more distinct keys than there are drops of water in the ocean. It would be impractical for someone to try them all one by one.

Despite this, it leaves patterns in the ciphertext that can be analyzed. With some trial and error, it's surprisingly easy to break the cipher, especially when a computer can help us count letters and recognize dictionary words. For example, in typical English texts, E is the most frequent letter. If the most frequent letter in the ciphertext is R, there's a good chance E → R is in the key. Furthermore, TH is the pair of letters that appears most often together in English. If ZN is the most frequent letter pair of the ciphertext, we can guess that T → Z and H → N.

This is called **frequency analysis**, and it provides a good starting point for testing different encryption keys. Try to use it to solve the following problem:

---

[2]The exclamation mark denotes a factorial: $26! = 26 \times 25 \times \cdots \times 2 \times 1$.

HOLLOW COIN 🪙 You found an old coin that seemed exceptionally light. You dropped it on the floor and it cracked open, revealing a tiny piece of paper. With a magnifying glass, you read the following note:

```
DUA KVYBVHA PVJ OAZQMASAO DW CWES PQLA
KASJWFVZZC. AMASCDUQFH QJ VZZ SQHUD PQDU
DUA LVGQZC. PA PQJU CWE JEYYAJJ. HSAADQFHJ
LSWG DUA YWGSVOAJ.
```

Can you break the cipher?

This task can feel daunting at first, but with a pen, paper and some patience, it is feasible. Since the plaintext is assumed to be English, we start by finding the encrypted letters that most likely stand for E and TH. Step by step, we compare half-solved words with common English words and see how different possible substitutions affect the rest of the text. One possible path to the solution is presented in Appendix III.

ADVANCED SUBSTITUTIONS Stronger substitution ciphers may convert a plaintext letter to different symbols. For instance, plaintext E could be replaced by either R, $, or *. By having more substitution options for the most frequent English letters, frequency analysis becomes more difficult. However, common words and letter pairs will still leave subtle patterns in the ciphertext. More symbols can be devised to replace letter pairs and common words, further thwarting frequency analysis—yet never defeating it.

Product Ciphers

A combination of ciphers is called a **product cipher**. They are most effective when ciphers that shuffle the plaintext are combined with ciphers that make substitutions. For example, a plaintext can go through the zigzag cipher and then through the simple substitution cipher. The resulting product cipher is stronger than any of its individual components.

Suppose TH is the most frequent letter pair of the plaintext, as expected for English texts. If TH is replaced for ZN, the most frequent letter pair of the ciphertext will *not* be **ZN**, due to the zigzag shuffling. However, the occurrence of a given ciphered letter always comes from the same plaintext letter, so frequency analysis is still possible.

During World War I, the Germans used a product cipher to communicate via radio. The cipher had a substitution step followed by a shuffling step. The Germans believed it was unbreakable. Yet, the French managed to break it and eavesdrop on their foes. By knowing German plans well in advance, the Allies were able to anticipate attacks and better manage their resources.

Vigenère Cipher

So far, we've seen ciphers that perform substitutions according to one mapping between ciphertext and plaintext letters. Stronger substitution ciphers use *multiple* mappings. One way to do this is by iterating over a list of shift ciphers for each successive letter of the plaintext. For instance, using the key **2-0-1-1-0-6-4**, we can replace letters as follows:[3]

```
T H E R E F O R E  T H E Y  L O A T H E D  T H E F T
2-0-1-1-0-6-4 2-0—1-1-0-6—4 2-0-1-1-0-6—4 2-0-1-1-
    ↓↓↓           ↓↓↓            ↓↓↓           ↓↓↓
V H F S E L S T E  U I E E  P Q A U I E J  X J E G U
```

This is called the **Vigenère cipher**. Notice that plaintext **E** letters can be encoded as **F**, **E**, **G**, **K** or **I**. Using longer keys, each plaintext letter has even more possible substitutions. As a result, the Vigenère cipher can mitigate the threat of frequency analysis. This cipher was invented in the 16th century, and remained unbroken for over 300 years. Many even believed it to be unbreakable.

Today, the Vigenère cipher can be easily broken by a computer.[4] By observing repeated sequences of letters in the ciphertext, it's possible to guess the length of the encryption key. For instance,

---

[3]Vigenère keys are often expressed with letters rather than numbers. This allows for shorter keys, as the numbers **0-25** are written using one character each (**A-Z**). For example, the key **17-24-15-19-14-2** can be written **RYPTOC**.

[4]The Vigenère cipher was first broken in 1845 by Charles Babbage—the same man who designed the first programmable computer back in 1837.

notice that in our example, the pattern UIE is repeated. The second occurrence appears seven positions after the first one:

V H F S E L S T E <u>U I E</u> E P Q A <u>U I E</u> J X J E G U
              1 2 3 4 5 6 7

It is likely that a pattern that appears twice in the same Vigenère ciphertext corresponds to a pattern that also appears twice in the original plaintext. However, this only happens if the distance between the two appearances is equal to a multiple of the length of the encryption key. Since the two UIE sequences appear seven positions apart, there is a good chance that the key has seven numbers. If, for example, they had been fifteen positions apart, it would have been a sign that the key had three, five or fifteen numbers.

Once we have guessed the length of the key, frequency analysis can be used. If the key length is seven, we start by retrieving every seventh letter of the ciphertext. In the resulting group of letters, we find the most frequent one: it is likely replacing the plaintext E.

Repeating this process with six more starting letters can be sufficient to break the cipher if the text is long enough. Even if the ciphertext is short like in our example, frequency analysis tells us the most probable keys to test, and the solution can be found with little computational power in today's standards.[5]

Vernam Cipher

The Vigenère cipher is the most secure when the encryption key has as many numbers as there are letters in the plaintext. We call this variation the **Vernam cipher**. Mathematicians have proven it is impossible to break the Vernam cipher, as long as the key is chosen at random and only used *once*. Otherwise, patterns emerge.

Consider the two ciphertexts VSXOCQZQCLGHQGBFHTJK and NHPJEXGPTDDBFCFOYKRA. If they were encrypted with the same Vernam encryption key, there's a trick we can apply. First, we choose a common word that is likely to be in the plaintext, which we call a **crib**. We assume the crib is in one of the plaintexts, and check how it affects the other. Let's try "tomorrow" as a crib:

---

[5]There's a tool to break Vigenère ciphertext at http://code.energy/vigenere.

Figure 3.1 If the first letter of plaintext 1 is T, the first number of the key must be 2, so that T → V. Under this assumption, the first letter of plaintext 2 must be L, so that L → N.

If "tomorrow" was at the start of the first plaintext, the second plaintext would have to start with "ldejtyvv". Assuming neither of the plaintexts contains gibberish, the word "tomorrow" can't be at the start of first plaintext. So we keep trying the crib at other positions. When trying the 7th position, we have a breakthrough:

```
ciphertext 1  V  S  X  O  C  Q  Z  Q  C  L  G  H  Q  G  B  F  H  T  J  K
                                   T  O  M  O  R  R  O  W
                                   6  2  16 23 15 16 2  10
ciphertext 2  N  H  P  J  E  X  G  P  T  D  D  B  F  C  F  O  Y  K  R  A
                                   A  N  D  G  O  L  D  S
```

Figure 3.2 Bingo! 🎉 By testing "tomorrow" in the seventh position of the first plaintext, we derive a key segment which decodes the other ciphertext to intelligible text rather than gibberish. This confirms the guess was correct.

This trick is called **crib-dragging**. In order to make the Vernam cipher immune to it, we should *never* use the same encryption key on two different plaintexts. For this reason, we typically call a Vernam cipher's encryption key a **one-time pad**.

In the 1940s, the Soviet Army sometimes reused one-time pads when transmitting Vernam ciphertexts. American intelligence managed to intercept their radio transmissions and eventually broke the code by crib-dragging. They discovered, among other things, that Soviet spies had infiltrated their nuclear weapons program.

To this day, the Vernam cipher is the gold standard for secret communications. It's the only cipher that's proven to be unbreakable if used properly. But it isn't very practical: parties must share an identical, large sequence of secret random numbers before they can start exchanging encrypted messages. A secure cipher that works with a shorter key would be much more versatile.

Cipher Machines

In the 1920s and 1930s, military powers around the world needed to quickly encrypt and decrypt messages without the hassle of sharing large encryption keys. Therefore, they designed machines that ran smaller forms of shared secrets among communicating parties as surrogates for the large keys. The new devices employed tricks that allowed short shared secrets to be continuously expanded into larger and larger encryption keys called **keystreams**.

These early cipher machines were made of successive wheels, each with their own intricate internal wiring (Figure 3.3). Before encrypting or decrypting each letter, the wheels moved in concert to a new position. At each position, their wirings would form a completely different circuit, expanding the keystream with a new *seemingly random* mapping.

Messages *seemed* like they were encrypted using infinitely long random encryption keys. In reality, the keystream was not random but **pseudorandom**: the same keystream could be reproduced at any time on a different copy of the machine. The only thing that was needed was the knowledge of the shared secret:[6] the initial position of the wheels.

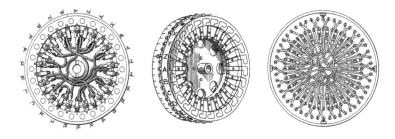

Figure 3.3 Cipher machine wheels. As they rotate, they form seemingly chaotic circuits in a deterministic and reproducible way.

---

[6]We often use the term *encryption key* to refer to the short shared secret rather than the keystream it produces.

Cipher machines were widely used in World War II, allowing messages to be encrypted and decrypted fast and using short shared secrets rather than long one-time pads. However, their keystreams displayed subtle patterns which were exploited by codebreakers on both sides. Teams of mathematicians and engineers worked around the clock to break intercepted ciphertexts.

All German cipher machines were broken before the war ended, even the model used by Hitler's high command. Meanwhile, the strongest American cipher machine, called SIGABA, was never broken. In recent years, it was proven that patterns will always emerge from a keystream generated by rotating wheels—meaning that even SIGABA was vulnerable.

Fortunately, computers allow us to operate even stronger ciphers. Let's now explore how they can go one step further than these analog cipher machines.

3.2   Symmetry

Today, almost all of our encryption relies on computers. Since our computers operate on binary data, we must design our ciphers for an alphabet of two symbols: 0 and 1. For instance, the Vernam cipher can work with a binary alphabet just as effectively as with a 26-letter alphabet:

Figure 3.4   Shifting binary plaintext with a binary one-time pad. When the digit 1 is shifted forward, it loops over and goes back to 0.[7]

Any information that's stored in a computer can be encrypted with perfect secrecy using the Vernam cipher. However, the inconvenience of one-time pads remains. To encrypt a gigabyte of video,

---

[7]This process is equivalent to sequential boolean XOR operations. You can learn more about boolean operations in our first book, *Computer Science Distilled*.

a gigabyte of secret random numbers is needed. And remember, one-time pads can't be reused: crib-dragging also works in binary!

Thankfully, there are secure ciphers that can encrypt large volumes of data using a relatively small shared secret. These ciphers are divided into two categories according to their underlying working mechanism. Let's take the simplest first.

Stream Ciphers

The first approach is to avoid long one-time pads in similar fashion to the cipher machines with rotary wheels. This time, however, we write a computer program that generates an endless stream of pseudorandom numbers. For example, given the non-square number 1337, a stream of seemingly unpredictable digits emerges as we calculate its square root:

$$\sqrt{1337} = 36.56\ 50\ 10\ 59\ 75\ 64\ 44\ 26\ 58\ 66\ 10\ 65\ 18\ 28...$$

This is a basic form of **P**seudo**R**andom **N**umber **G**enerator (**PRNG**). A PRNG requires a **seed** to serve as its starting point, similarly to the shared secret that described the initial position of a legacy cipher machine's wheels. In our example, the seed is 1337.

Stream ciphers rely on PRNGs to generate keystreams. Let's take our example and group digits after the decimal point in pairs to generate a stream of pseudorandom numbers between 0 and 99:

Figure 3.5 Vernam cipher running on a pseudorandom number generator. The shared secret between the parties is just the seed.[8]

Today, stream ciphers generally use PRNGs that directly generate a stream of binary digits. The PRNG algorithm is the foundation

---

[8]Here, it was also agreed that 26 corresponds to a shift of 0 positions, 27 corresponds to a shift of 1, etc.

and the defining element of a stream cipher. A stream cipher is only secure if its PRNG outputs pseudorandom numbers with no detectable patterns. Even if they knew which PRNG to use, it should be impossible for parties without the shared secret to distinguish the PRNG's output from a sequence of truly random coin flips.

To this day, we don't know if an invulnerable PRNG exists. Vulnerabilities were found in many PRNGs proposed by experts in the past. Before picking a stream cipher, check which ones are vetted by experts, for which no vulnerabilities are known.[9] Designing a good PRNG is extremely challenging, so unless you want to become a cryptographer yourself, we recommend you stick to existing ones.

NONCE Since keystreams have the same purpose as one-time pads, they should never be used more than once. A PRNG will always generate the same keystream when given the same seed, so a seed should never be reused. If the shared secret is directly used as the seed, communicating parties have to be able to agree on a new one before each communication. This can be impractical, therefore cryptographers devised a trick that allows us to reuse a shared secret. The trick uses a **nonce**: an arbitrary, single-use, non-secret number that is combined with the shared secret to generate a seed.

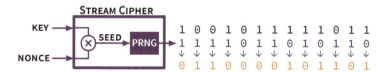

Figure 3.6 Stream ciphers typically require a shared secret (referred to as the key) and a nonce. Unlike the key, the nonce doesn't need to be secret. If nonces are never reused, a key can be used to encrypt multiple plaintexts.

Before you encrypt anything with a stream cipher, you must pick a nonce. If you pick a random number, make sure you're unlikely to pick it again in the future. For example, you can generate a random 64-bit number: since there are more than a hundred million *trillion*

---

[9]Check the recommended ciphers here: http://code.energy/stream.

different possibilities, the chance of picking the same nonce twice is almost zero.

When transmitting a message encrypted with a stream cipher, send the unencrypted nonce along with the ciphertext. The receiver will first combine the incoming nonce with the key, then recreate the artificial one-time pad, and finally shift back the ciphertext to obtain the plaintext. Even if hackers intercept many ciphertexts and know each of their nonces, they will not be able to detect any patterns between them since they each were encrypted with their own keystream!

KEY SELECTION An attacker that intercepts your ciphertext can try to break it by brute-force: trying all possible keys until an intelligible plaintext is found. Be pessimistic: assume your attacker knows which cipher you are using and has multiple times the entire computing power of the world. If you select a long enough random encryption key, you insure yourself against any possible brute-force attack. For instance, a 120-bit random key leaves a powerful attacker no chance of brute-forcing your ciphertexts.[10]

MALLEABILITY ATTACK Suppose Ada sends an encrypted message to her bank requesting a $100 transfer to Andrew's account; and suppose the message follows a standard format, where bits 5 to 9 encode the destination account number. Suppose Charles knows all that, and is in charge of transmitting the encrypted message from Ada to the bank. If Charles knows that Andrew's bank account number is 1001, he can change Ada's message so that the deposit goes to his own account number, 11100:

					0	1	0	0	1	Andrew's account number						
Original ciphertext	0	1	1	1	0	1	1	1	1	1	0	0	0	1	1	0
					0	0	1	1	0	key segment						
					1	1	1	0	0	Charles' account number						
Forged ciphertext	0	1	1	1	1	1	0	1	0	1	0	0	0	1	1	0

[10]To have a 0.1% chance of guessing a 120-bit random key, an attacker would have to try 106 billion keys per second for 400 trillion years—almost thirty thousand times the age of the universe.

If an attacker can forge parts of the ciphertext only by knowing corresponding parts of the plaintext, we say that the cipher is malleable. We can devise ciphers that aren't malleable, as we'll see next.

Block Ciphers

With stream ciphers, there's always a clear relationship between plaintext and ciphertext: if you flip the tenth bit of the plaintext (changing it to 1 if it's a 0 and to a 0 if it's a 1), it will cause the tenth bit of the ciphertext to flip. Having this relationship is not ideal. In fact, the malleability of stream ciphers is a consequence of it. A cipher is more secure if it produces no obvious relationship between ciphertext and plaintext.

Recall the legacy product cipher that combined the zigzag and simple substitution ciphers. It was stronger because the zigzag shuffling diffused the relationship between ciphertext and plaintext. But the zigzag cipher doesn't do enough: ideally, the link between plaintext and ciphertext should be so diffused that changing a single bit of the plaintext would cause the entire ciphertext to change.

When using stream ciphers, changing one bit of the key leads to a completely different ciphertext. Since the Second World War, cryptographers have been developing ciphers for which changing a single bit of *either* the key *or* the plaintext entails a transformation of the entire ciphertext.

This goal can be achieved using a product cipher that combines substitution and shuffling operations. However, ridding it from *all* observable malleability across different chunks of the ciphertext is not straightforward: the product cipher has to be applied multiple times, and its substitution and shuffling operations must be carefully chosen. In fact, operations for a suitable product cipher could only be found under the constraint that the plaintext always has the same *fixed size*.

Ciphers that operate on this principle are called **block ciphers**, because the plaintext must be encrypted in fixed-size blocks. If the plaintext is longer than the block size, it has to be divided into multiple chunks. If a plaintext isn't long enough to fill an entire block, it is typically padded with zeros. Currently, the most commonly used block ciphers work with blocks of 128 or 256 bits.

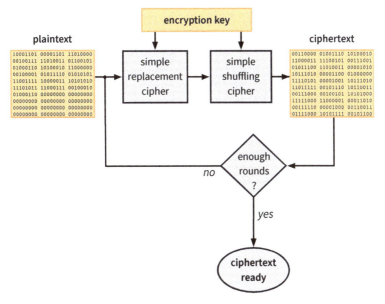

Figure 3.7 Simplified schematic of a block cipher. Typically, block ciphers must iterate their core product cipher about a dozen times.

Block ciphers aren't malleable. If one bit is changed in a block of ciphertext, then the entire message gets decrypted into garbled data. For this reason, even if bits of the plaintext are known, the attacker is unable to alter the ciphertext and create a forged message.

There are several ways to split and encrypt plaintexts that are longer than the block size. The simplest way to do it is to split and pad the plaintext into blocks of the right size and then to directly apply the block cipher to each one of them. We say that the resulting ciphertext was encrypted in Electronic Codebook (ECB) mode.

Unfortunately, there's a problem with ECB: an attacker can know if the same block of plaintext is encrypted twice using the same key, as that will result in the exact same block of ciphertext. For example, if an attacker knows that a block of ciphertext tells a bank to credit $100 dollars to his account, he could potentially replay that message again every time he wants an extra $100.

And beware: this vulnerability can also allow an attacker to obtain information about a long plaintext encrypted in ECB mode. For example, suppose we wish to encrypt an image file. When we split sections of the image file into blocks of plaintext, sections of identical shade and color will yield identical blocks of ciphertext:

 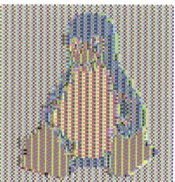

Figure 3.8 An image encrypted using a block cipher in ECB mode. Patterns of plaintext (left) are repeated, and the disposition of those repeated blocks in the ciphertext (right) reveal the nature of its content.

To fix this, we transform the plaintext to ensure every plaintext block has a unique value. There are many ways to do it. One way is to use a nonce as large as the size of a block, called the Initialization Vector (**IV**):

- We start by transforming the first block of plaintext by applying the nonce as if it were a one-time pad (as demonstrated at the beginning of this section). This transformed plaintext is then properly encrypted with the block cipher key.
- For each subsequent block, we use the previous block of ciphertext as the one-time pad to transform the plaintext. Each transformed plaintext can then be safely encrypted with the same block cipher key.

When a block cipher is used this way, we say it's being operated in Cipher Block Chaining (**CBC**) mode. You won't need to code any of these plaintext transformations yourself. Instead, you can configure your cryptographic library to make your block cipher operate using the mode you want. There are other modes that avoid the pitfalls of ECB mode, but unless you know what you're doing, we recommend you stick to CBC mode!

As with stream ciphers, vulnerabilities have been found in many of the block ciphers proposed by experts so far. Before you select a block cipher to use, check which ones are currently recommended by cryptographers.[11]

BLOCK CIPHER VS STREAM CIPHER Block ciphers require more computing power than stream ciphers. When the extra security of the block ciphers isn't required, and the plaintext is being created dynamically (e.g. live encryption of a phone call), it can be better to choose a stream cipher. They allow the plaintext to be encrypted and transmitted one byte at a time, whereas block ciphers require larger chunks of data to be encrypted before transmission.

Stream ciphers and block ciphers are part of a larger category called **symmetric ciphers**, because they require both communication parties to have a copy of the same key. In other words, you can only secure a communication with a symmetric cipher if you have previously agreed on a shared secret with your counterpart.

3.3   Asymmetry

Before we can communicate using a symmetric cipher, we must find a secure way to share a secret encryption key with our correspondent. In the past, people had to meet in person or send keys through a trusted courier. Today, there are ways for two people who have never met to share a secret key *without* using a secure communication link.

Diffie–Hellman Key Exchange

Suppose Ada wants to send a secret message to Charles, but they haven't yet decided on a shared secret. There's a technique, called the **Diffie–Hellman** key exchange, that allows Ada and Charles to jointly select a secret number. It only requires them to send each

---

[11]Currently, the best recommended block ciphers are AES and Twofish with block sizes of 256 bits.

other a message *that doesn't even have to be secret*. From these public messages, it's impossible for a third party to know which secret number Ada and Charles selected. Let's see how it works:

1. Ada chooses a prime number p and some other arbitrary number g. She then picks a secret number a that she won't share.
2. Ada sends a message to Charles containing p, g, and a third number A calculated using the *modulo* operation:[12]

$$A = g^a \mod p.$$

3. Charles picks a secret number c, and sends a message to Ada containing the number C, computed as follows:

$$C = g^c \mod p.$$

4. Ada computes $C^a \mod p$, and Charles computes $A^c \mod p$. By some amazing math properties, they both computed the same number! In other words, their shared secret is:

$$C^a \mod p \quad = \quad A^c \mod p,$$

where Ada is the only one to know a and Charles is the only one to know c.

For this scheme to be secure, the numbers must be large: a, c, g and p must be chosen such that each number is several hundred digits long. Also, the secret numbers a and c must be chosen at random. If these requisites are met, there isn't any viable method for attackers to discover the shared secret key without knowledge of either a or c.

There is still, however, a security risk that is not covered by the Diffie–Hellman key exchange: how can Ada and Charles be sure that they're really interacting with each other? Maybe, Ada receives C *not* from Charles, but from an attacker impersonating him. Fortunately, cryptographers developed tools that can address this problem.

---

[12] $a \mod b$ is the remainder of $a \div b$. For example, $27 \mod 10 = 7$, because when we divide 27 into 10, the remainder is 7.

Public Key Ciphers

Ciphers we've seen so far use the same key for encryption and decryption. Inspired by Diffie and Hellman, cryptographers developed a different type of cipher, where a second key is derived from the main key. Whoever knows the second key can perform the encryption operation. However, decryption requires the main key. Ciphers that use different keys for encryption and decryption are **asymmetric ciphers**.

With symmetric ciphers there's only one key, which is known by everyone involved in the secret conversation. The key is only useful to that group of people and it must always be a *shared secret*. With asymmetric ciphers, there are two keys. The main key is the **private key**, and it is only known to one person (or entity). The second key is the **public key**, and it is ideally available to everyone. One pair of private–public keys can serve many different communication contexts.

Suppose Charles wants to communicate with Ada. If Charles knows Ada's public key, he can use it to encrypt his plaintext message. He then transmits the ciphertext to Ada, and Ada can use her private key to decrypt it. If Andrew also wants to communicate with Ada, he can follow the same process, effectively using the same pair of keys in a different context! However, if Ada wants to respond to both of them, she will have to use Charles' public key to encrypt the message for Charles and Andrew's public key to encrypt the message for Andrew.

There are still pitfalls when using public key ciphers. For instance, when Ada receives ciphertext from Charles, how can Ada be sure that the message really came from Charles and not an impostor? Ada's public key is *public*, so anyone can send her a ciphertext claiming to be Charles. Secondly, if Charles is unable to physically meet with Ada, how can he retrieve a copy of her key and ensure that the key is legitimate?

Digital Signatures

Besides encryption and decryption, two more operations based on asymmetric cryptography were created: **signing** and **verifying**.

The signing operation takes a plaintext and a private key as inputs and outputs a big number called a **digital signature**. The verifying operation takes a public key, a plaintext and a digital signature as inputs, and outputs `true` or `false` depending on the legitimacy of the digital signature.

The only way to produce a legitimate digital signature for a given plaintext and public key is to perform the signing operation with the matching private key. Remember, with asymmetric cryptography, private keys are associated with an individual. Using your private key to produce a digital signature for a given plaintext is the digital equivalent of scribbling your signature next to the plaintext. The only difference is that a traditional signature always looks the same, and a digital signature looks *completely* different for each new plaintext—even if a single letter is changed.

Compute a digital signature and publish it along with the message, and anyone who knows your public key will be able to perform the verifying operation and attest that you created that signature for that message. While fraudsters routinely forge physical signatures, nobody has figured out how to forge a digital signature made with strong cryptography.

Digital signatures enable us to securely communicate with anyone, even if attackers are meddling with communication links. Recall the Diffie–Hellman key exchange: the only issue was that participants can't be sure the numbers they're sending each other weren't modified in transit by attackers. When the messages in the key exchange are accompanied by digital signatures, there's no way an impostor can undermine the process. If an attacker meddles with the messages, the digital signatures don't match, and people can know they're being duped before any information is exchanged.

RSA & ECDSA In 2020, the mostly widely used asymmetric cryptographic schemes are RSA and ECDSA.[13] RSA is more versatile: its key pairs can be used for both encrypting/decrypting and signing/verifying. ECDSA is computationally less expensive, but can only be used for signing/verifying. The working mechanisms of

---

[13]RSA stands for Rivest–Shamir–Adleman and ECDSA stands for Elliptic Curve Digital Signature Algorithm.

both schemes are based on advanced mathematics. Follow the specific instructions to operate each of these schemes, and you'll be secure. For instance, when signing with ECDSA, you must always provide a nonce. If you reuse one, your security will be weak!

Digital Certificates

Imagine Charles wants to send a secret message to Ada, but he doesn't know her public key. If Ada sends her key to Charles through an insecure link, attackers could intercept the message and change it so that Charles receives their key instead. If he falls for the trap, their communications will be decipherable to the attackers.

Suppose Charles knows the public key of his trusted friend Louis, and Louis has a copy of Ada's public key. Louis can help by publishing a message with Ada's key followed by the statement: "I, Louis, attest that this public key is Ada's." He then digitally signs this message, and makes the message and signature public. Now, anyone who trusts Louis and has a copy of his public key can retrieve the message and verify the signature. If the signature is valid, then they can trust that the copy of Ada's key in his message is legitimate—without having ever met her!

A message stating that a given person or organization has a given public key is called a **digital certificate**. A broadly trusted entity that creates and signs digital certificates is called a Certificate Authority (**CA**). Verisign is one of the best accredited CAs. In fact, most computers come out of the box with Verisign's public key recorded alongside the operating system. If you get Verisign to sign a digital certificate with your public key, you can send both (certificate and key) through an insecure link to virtually anyone, and they will be able to verify its authenticity.

Asymmetric ciphers are thousands of times more computationally demanding than symmetric ciphers. For this reason, it's mostly used for people to validate each other's public keys with digital certificates and to establish symmetric encryption keys with signed Diffie–Hellman messages. Next, let's see how we can make signing and verifying long messages less computationally demanding.

3.4 Hashing

In the first chapter, we discovered checksums: functions that take any input and produce a fixed-length output number. If a single bit of the input changes, the checksum computes a different output. With the aid of cryptography, special checksum functions can be crafted such that it's infeasible to find an input for which the function computes a specific output. These special methods are called **cryptographic hash functions**, and an output of such a function is commonly called a **hash**.

Figure 3.9 Hashing a sample file. This hash function produces a binary number with 256 bits as output, represented in hexadecimal. It's infeasible to find a different input that produces the same output.

Hash functions are computationally inexpensive, and this property can facilitate the implementation of digital signatures. Rather than performing the computationally expensive task of signing a large file, we can quickly run it through a hash function and sign the output. The signature is secure because potential attackers won't be able to create another file that has the same hash. Today, almost every signature is calculated over a hash of the signed data. There are several other ways hash functions are used. Let's explore a few.

Malicious Change Detection

Simple checksums are used to detect whether accidental changes were made to a given chunk of data. However, they don't help to catch malicious alterations made by experienced attackers: with some effort, they can forge data that has the same checksum as the original data.

CELESTIAL SECURITY 🔭 Your laboratory's supercomputer stores data from celestial observations. You suspect someone is changing your data late at night in order to sabotage your research. The files are large: you can't make a private copy of every file. How can you ensure your data isn't being maliciously altered?

The solution is straightforward: choose a hash function, and compute the hash of every file. Record all hashes in a pen drive that you take home. If you suspect the files have changed, calculate their hashes again. If they are the same as the ones in your pen drive, you can be certain not a single bit has been changed. That is, unless the adversary has managed break the security of the hash function you're using. Later we'll see what makes a hash function secure.

Message Authentication Code

A **M**essage **A**uthentication **C**ode (**MAC**)[14] is a way to prove a given message originated from someone who has knowledge of a specific key. While a MAC can be implemented with digital signatures, it's computationally faster to implement it using hash functions.

SECURE SURVEY 📇 You'll conduct a survey targeting millions of respondents. You plan to send a unique survey code to each respondent, saying something like this: "This person is eligible to answer the survey as ■", where ■ is filled according to the name or the ID of each respondent. How can you allow only the people who received a legitimate survey code to answer your survey?

If you only send the plain message quoted above, attackers could alter the message and insert whatever data they want! The simplest way to curb these attacks is to add a large random number to each survey code and keep records of all the codes you send out. When a stranger presents a survey code with a large random number, you consult your database to determine if you indeed issued that survey code. This solution is cumbersome because you'd have to keep track of millions of codes.

---

[14]Not to be confused with MAC in networking, which stands for *medium access control* (see sec. 1.1).

With asymmetric encryption, you could use digital signatures and send each respondent a signed survey code. This way, you don't have to keep any records. When a code is presented with its signature, you verify your own signature in order to determine whether you created that survey code.

There's another way to achieve the same outcome, but using a hash function. First, you generate a random secret key. You store it carefully and you don't share it with anyone. For each respondent, you use the secret key to calculate the following:[15]

```
msg ← "Eligible to answer as " + respondent_name
mac ← hash(secret_key + msg)
```

A survey code can be created by joining `msg` and `mac`. When someone presents a code, you extract the `msg` part and use your secret key to recalculate `mac`. If the `mac` number you calculated is exactly the same as the one in the survey code you were presented, the code is authentic.[16]

MACs are useful for people communicating through stream ciphers. Remember: messages encrypted with any stream cipher are vulnerable to malleability attacks. If a MAC is added at the end of the message using the encryption key as the secret, the recipient can recalculate the MAC and verify that the message hasn't been tampered with.

Password Handling

Most computer systems authenticate users by requesting them to enter a password. This means that they must store records of all passwords. But keeping plaintext copies of passwords is terrible practice: if the system is hacked, the passwords of every user can potentially be known to the hackers. In addition, many people have the bad habit of reusing their passwords, so such a security breach in one system can lead to breaches in other systems.

Storing encrypted passwords doesn't solve the problem. With complete access to a system, attackers can potentially find the key

---

[15]Here, + is the concatenation operation: "code" + "energy" = "codeenergy".

[16]Depending on the hash function, the MAC might have to be calculated as `hash(key + hash(key + msg))` rather than `hash(key + msg)`. Use a cryptographic library to generate MACs and ensure they're calculated properly.

and figure out how the system automatically encrypts or decrypts passwords when verifying login attempts. At this point, everyone's encrypted password can then potentially be decrypted!

For this reason, it's better to store the hash of each password rather than an encrypted copy: contrarily to ciphers, hash functions are not reversible. However, you can still check the password provided at login by hashing it and comparing it to the hash you're storing. If the hashes are the same, the password is correct.[17] Yet, even if a computer system is only storing password hashes, there's still a way for attackers to know people's passwords.

DICTIONARY ATTACK Attackers can compute the hashes of trillions of arbitrary passwords and create a sort of dictionary that maps hashes *back* to plaintext passwords. Stolen password hashes can then be looked up in this dictionary. This is a sort of brute force attack, but the work has to be done only once. It's effective because most people use simple passwords. In 2012, a hacker attacked LinkedIn and leaked the password hashes of over 6 million people; and a dictionary attack could reveal most of them. Storing password hashes can be almost as bad as storing plain copies of the passwords.

SALTING Fortunately, there is a way to prevent dictionary attacks. Instead of saving the result of `hash(password)` to a database, the system can generate a random number called a **salt** and store it in plaintext along with the result of `hash(password+salt)`. Since each user has a different salt, this forces the attackers to try and brute force each password hash individually. Every time they try to find the password of a given user, they don't even know if that user has a simple password that would take minutes to brute force or a complicated one that could take centuries.

MULTIPLE HASHING ROUNDS There's a way to make things even harder for attackers attempting to brute force password hashes. Instead of calculating and storing the hash of the password, we calculate and store the hash *of that hash*. In other words, we store

---

[17]This is why computer systems with proper security will *never* email you your password during a recovery process: they don't even know what it is!

the result of `hash(hash(password+salt))`. An attacker then needs about twice the time to guess the correct password. We can add as many rounds of hashing as we wish. Since calculating a hash is fast, some systems perform thousands of hashing rounds. Remember: if you're storing password hashes, make sure you're using salts and performing multiple rounds of hashing.

Proof of Existence

Hash functions can be used to create proofs that some information exists, without revealing any part of the information itself.

> SECRETIVE STAR You've composed an amazing song that you believe will be the next "Hotel California". You want to keep the music secret and only release it in your next album, but you're scared someone might steal the song. You want the song notarized, but you'd prefer not revealing the song even to the notary. How can you prove you created a song without revealing it?

The first step is to record the song to a computer file. You then calculate the hash of the file, and ask a notary to record that hash number. If the authorship of the song is contested, you can reveal your notarized hash number, along with the song recording. The only way you could have requested a notary to certify that specific hash number is by having possession of the recording file.

Online gambling sites also utilize hashing to prove to their clients that each game is fair. Imagine a simple game where one bets on the result of a coin toss. If you correctly call the toss, you double your stake; if you don't, you lose all of it. First, the online casino asks you for a number and randomly generates a coin toss. Suppose it's heads. The casino then calculates:

```
hash("HEADS" + user_salt + house_salt)
```

The `house_salt` number is chosen by the house and `user_salt` by you. The house presents you the hash and then waits for your guess. If you lose, the house can prove it didn't cheat you by disclosing their `house_salt`. You can then recalculate the hash, and check that it matches the hash provided by the house before you guessed. The house can't cheat! To check that you understood the principle, try to answer the following question: why can't the house also tell you their `house_salt` number *before* you guess?[18]

Proof of Work

If you continuously calculate hash numbers for different inputs, eventually you'll have an output that matches any specific pattern. For instance, if you are looking for a hash that starts with four zeros in binary, you can iterate as follows:

```
hash("heads1")  → 10111100000101101000011010010001...
hash("heads2")  → 11011001100111011000011110110000...
hash("heads3")  → 01110000011010011111110000101110...
hash("heads4")  → 11000101000110000011010110100000...
hash("heads5")  → 11101110000011110111101111100011...
hash("heads6")  → 11001001011010101011010011001011...
hash("heads7")  → 11000001001100101101101010010101...
hash("heads8")  → 01001111100001010110100111111000...
hash("heads9")  → 00111011011110101100010101010111...
hash("heads10") → 11101110000111111101000101101001...
hash("heads11") → 10101011110111001100000111111001...
hash("heads12") → 11101000110010001110100001001001...
hash("heads13") → 00100100001011011101101101000100...
hash("heads14") → 01111100010000100101101011000000...
hash("heads15") → 00101110000011100011001001100000...
hash("heads16") → 01010001000001011111011000000000...
hash("heads17") → 11110011000111011100001001101111...
hash("heads18") → 00111010001011001001100100110110...
hash("heads19") → 00100111100101110100011010000110...
hash("heads20") → 10111101011010100010011111110001...
hash("heads21") → 10110010100010110001000111000010...
hash("heads22") → 01111000100001111111010010001000...
hash("heads23") → 10101111001001011100100001110000...
hash("heads24") → 01110011110010011101111001101011...
hash("heads25") → 00100010101101110000111000110110...
hash("heads26") → 00001110001101011100100110011111...
```

---

[18] If you know both salts in advance, you can easily brute-force the hash before making your guess, as there are only two hashes you have to calculate: the one for heads and the one for tails!

After 26 different hash calculations, we come across the hash of `heads26`. This number, written in binary, begins with four zeros! Now imagine someone presented you the following:

```
hash("heads750")  →  00000000101110000101101011101000…
```

Here, the hash begins with *eight* zeros! You can assume that whoever presented you with `heads750` had to commit at least some computational resources to calculate many hashes in order to find an input that produced a hash with such a pattern. We call this a **proof of work**. Even more work has probably been spent in order to find the following input, as its hash begins with 12 zeros:

```
hash("heads11759")  →  00000000000001110100001001001…
```

Proof of work can be used to make attacks more difficult. For example, by requesting users to present proof of work before making a request, a server can make it more expensive for attackers to overload it with bogus requests. The attackers would have to spend a lot of computational resources in order to create piles of requests that the server would accept to process.

BLOCKCHAIN Along with digital signatures and hashing, proof of work gave rise to a technology that is set to change the world: the blockchain! Over the next few years, we believe it can provide economic sovereignty to billions of people by eliminating middlemen and adding more transparency, privacy and accountability to our society. Along with blockchain, entirely new cryptographic tools with fancy names are being developed, such as "zero-knowledge proofs" and "homomorphic encryption". We can only dream of the power that will be unleashed by these technologies in the future!

Insecure Hash Functions

When two different inputs cause a hash function to produce the same output, we say there is a **collision**. With secure hash functions, the only way to obtain one is brute force: calculating the hashes of many different inputs until a collision appears by chance.

When hash functions produce outputs of more than 200 bits, it's infeasible to find collisions by brute force.[19] For all hash functions currently considered secure, there are no known collisions. Every so often, a hash function loses its status because cryptographers discover a method to find collisions that doesn't rely solely on brute force. As soon as such a method is discovered for a hash function, we immediately consider it insecure.

This happened to the MD5 and the SHA1 hash functions, which were considered secure in the 1990s. A decade later, methods to reduce the operations required to find collisions were discovered for both. Currently, there are only a handful of hash functions deemed secure by cryptographers. As of 2021, the most widely used is SHA2, and it has remained unbroken for two decades. However, keep in mind that this could change in the future. If you're using a hash function for something potentially sensitive, stay informed so you can react early if a new attack method is discovered.

3.5   Protocols

As you will recall from the previous chapter, all data traveling inside IP packets is potentially public information. Hackers who infiltrate telecom companies can alter IP packets traveling to and from their targets in order to undermine their communications.[20] We can protect ourselves against these dangers using cryptography. Typically, secure communication over the Internet involves these steps:

1. Obtain the authentic public key of your counterpart.
2. Generate a shared secret key with your counterpart using Diffie–Hellman. Verify that the messages you receive are authentic using the public key from step 1.
3. Encrypt all further communications with a symmetric cipher using the shared secret key from step 2.

---

[19]If a hash function outputs 200-bit numbers, that's 2^{200} different possible hash values. If you took the number of all grains of sand on earth, and multiplied that by a trillion a few times, you wouldn't even be remotely close to 2^{200}. Imagine trying to find a specific grain of sand in such a search space.

[20]In 2013, Edward Snowden revealed that the NSA has already mounted such attacks even against leaders of allied countries.

When the parties know each other's public key, it's possible to communicate securely with an asymmetric cipher directly, without resorting to a Diffie–Hellman key exchange. However, doing so creates a weakness: an attacker who discovers a private key can also decrypt all previous messages received by the victim, including with other people. By generating a fresh Diffie–Hellman secret for each communication session, an attacker who stole a private key will be unable to decrypt ciphertexts from previous sessions. A communication scheme with this property is said to have **forward secrecy**.

Many details must be observed in order to properly encrypt our communications with forward secrecy. For example, if a nonce is inadvertently reused or pseudorandom numbers are generated carelessly, the entire communication becomes vulnerable to attack. To avoid these problems, several security protocols have been widely adopted. These protocols define processes for people to communicate and to perform the necessary cryptographic steps in a rigid process, which mitigates the risk of mistakes.

Secure Access

In the early days of the Internet, hosts running a Telnet server typically accepted connections from strangers and would only ask for a password before handing over remote access to the shell. This provided almost no security: that password would travel through the Internet in plaintext.

In 1995, a protocol called **S**ecure **Sh**ell (**SSH**) was created to replace Telnet and address its shortcomings. Each server that accepts SSH connections must have a pair of private–public keys. In order to guarantee security, a client computer should know in advance the public key of the server it wants to connect to.[21]

By default, SSH servers expect connections on TCP port 22. After a client establishes a connection, the server sends its public key along with the cryptographic tools that it supports for encryption, hashing, and Message Authentication Code (MAC). The client

---

[21] In many cases, the person or organization operating the client computer also owns the server, so this task is as easy as copy-pasting the server's key on a pen drive. In other cases, the client's user must obtain the public key from a trusted source, and the security risks are the same as for any public key cipher.

compares the public key it just received with the one it was expecting. A mismatch of the public keys either means that the server has been reconfigured or that someone is tampering with the IP packets as they travel between the parties. The client must then abort the connection attempt and investigate which one of these is the cause.

If the public key is correct, the client checks the available cryptographic tools indicated by the server and selects which ones to use. The client sends the server its choice along with the first Diffie–Hellman message. The server answers with a signed Diffie–Hellman response. If the signature is valid, client and server calculate a shared secret key and begin communicating using the chosen symmetric cipher. At this point, the client can securely send a password in encrypted form. Once the connection is closed, client and server forget their shared key in order to maintain forward secrecy.

Secure Transport

Early Internet users didn't trust their Web browsers to deal with things that required high levels of security, such as online banking. Their concern was justified: with HTTP, information inside IP packets traveled in plaintext. Therefore, engineers set out to integrate encryption schemes into HTTP so that people could safely send sensitive information such as credit card numbers and private messages from inside their Web browsers.

They developed a generic protocol called **Transport Layer Security (TLS)**[22] that can secure *any* TCP connection. Its working mechanism is similar to SSH. First, the client presents a list of cryptographic tools it supports and a random number. In response, the server sends its public key, the selection of tools to be used, and another random number. The client checks if the public key is authentic. Client and server calculate a shared secret key and start sending each other ciphertexts using the cipher chosen by the server.

Contrarily to SSH, the client is not expected to know the public key of the server in advance. The server sends its public key along

---

[22]At its inception in 1995, the protocol was called **Secure Sockets Layer (SSL)**. As the protocol was upgraded, it was renamed to **Transport Layer Security (TLS)**, but many still refer to it by its older name or by SSL/TLS.

with a digital certificate. For example, if the server is hosted at example.com, it must send a public key, plus a digital certificate from a Certificate Authority (CA) attesting that example.com uses that public key.

After these steps, encrypted HTTP messages can be exchanged between client and server. When TLS is used with HTTP, we call the resulting protocol **HTTPS**. While HTTP uses port 80 by default, HTTPS defaults to port 443. Web servers listening to TCP port 443 expect the client to send the first TLS message right after the connection is established.

TLS is used in several other protocols besides HTTPS, including SMTP. There are programming libraries that make it easy for coders to use TCP with TLS. Instead of creating a regular TCP socket and manually securing it, the coder uses the library's functions to directly create a TLS socket. Behind the scenes, the library takes care of all the encryption work. Programmers can operate TLS sockets almost exactly as they would operate TCP sockets.

Other Protocols

Many more security protocols exist. For instance, IPsec is a protocol extension that provides security to IP-based communications. Contrarily to IP packets, IPsec packets can't be read or altered while they travel. IPsec is often used to create **V**irtual **P**rivate **N**etworks (**VPN**s), where an Internet connection acts as a physical link so that a computer can join a distant local network as if it were there.

DNS also has its own secure extension, called DNSSEC, that extends DNS records with digital signatures. This enables anyone to verify that a signed DNS record was created by its owner. Without DNSSEC, a DNS server can send you forged DNS records in order to direct you towards a malicious host. As of 2020, DNSSEC isn't widely used, but adoption is improving steadily.

Protocols for securing wireless communications are widely used. For example, they prevent people with radio sniffers from reading the contents of your IP packets transmitted via secure WiFi. They also allow you to type on a wireless Bluetooth keyboard without the risk of your keystrokes being recorded by an unauthorized machine.

Today, the lack of email security is a big concern. Emails can be transmitted securely using SMTP with TLS, but the vast majority of mail servers store emails in plaintext. Large email providers such as Gmail or Hotmail may read the emails of their users if they wish. Most security experts agree that a message should only be readable by its sender and recipient. Communication systems that adhere to this principle are said to use **end-to-end** encryption. Some instant messaging applications—such as Signal, Threema and WhatsApp—use end-to-end encryption. New protocols are being developed actively to make end-to-end encryption widely available for email.

3.6   Hacking

A **hacker** is a person with strong computer skills who is able to achieve certain goals in non-standard ways. In popular culture, hackers are often portrayed as geeky wizards who can infiltrate military-grade computer systems with a few keystrokes. Although movies aren't always realistic, there is some truth to the idea that hackers are an elite force. Hackers are often specialized in low-level computing and understand in detail each step a computer takes to execute a simple action.

Most of the time, hackers are IT security specialists who have a deep understanding of network protocols and are capable of manipulating individual bits in network packets. They use their skills to uncover loopholes that allow them to **pwn** a machine[23]—to gain control over it and perform tasks without permission.

This doesn't mean that all hackers are bad guys. **White hat** hackers work hard to ensure no harm is caused by vulnerabilities they uncover. They mostly search for vulnerabilities in order to fix them before any harm is done. In contrast, **black hat** hackers typically exploit vulnerabilities for personal gain regardless of the harm they cause in the process.

---

[23]*Pwning* is the cyber-slang spelling of *owning*: utterly defeating or destroying an adversary. It often refers to the successful hacking of a system or the leaking of sensitive data. For reference, the website *Have I Been Pwned?* will check if personal data associated with a given email address has ever been made public. Check it out at http://haveibeenpwned.com.

Typically, a hacker looks for ways to *bypass* (rather than break) the cryptography that protects a computer system. Designing a computer system is like building a medieval castle. You must anticipate how different attackers might attempt to infiltrate your castle and implement countermeasures for each attack vector. Knowing how hackers operate will help you to develop these countermeasures. Surprisingly, the most widely used hacking methods involve almost no technical skills.

Social Engineering

Hacking attacks most often take advantage of flaws of humans rather than computers. Tricking someone who has access to a computer system can be much easier than bypassing the defenses of the system itself. Malicious hackers typically do it by impersonating others through emails, phone calls and text messages. Sophisticated attackers sometimes counterfeit entire websites. Others will even physically show up at a data center impersonating an employee! These are called **social engineering** attacks.

Figure 3.10   Courtesy of http://smbc-comics.com.

Social engineers operate like con artists: they can develop elaborate schemes in order to gain trust and access. The most common trick is called **phishing**. It's when the attacker forges an email that appears to come from a trusted source. Phishing emails typically link to a counterfeit website requesting secret information such as a password or credit card number. More sophisticated ones will contain malicious software hidden within an attachment.

THE DNC PHISHING During the 2016 United States presidential election, hostile hackers crafted a phishing email directed to a member of the DNC.[24] The email warned of suspect Google account activity and urged the user to change the password. It included a link to a fake Google web page asking for the user's login details. As soon as the user entered the password, the attackers got in and downloaded thousands of sensitive emails. Most of them were leaked to the public, causing considerable political damage and the resignation of several key politicians.

Attacks like these keep happening time and again. It's estimated that about 90% of all data leaks originate from a successful phishing attack. There's also a variant of this attack vector called **vishing**: the hacker impersonates someone on the phone in order to obtain privileged information or access to computer systems.

THE CIA VISHING In 2015, a 15-year-old British hacker called Verizon and pretended to be a staff employee. He managed to obtain key information about a special Verizon customer: the director of the CIA.[25] Using this information, the hacker was then able to impersonate the director himself on a call with AOL tech support. He correctly answered all security questions, and changed the director's email password. Ultimately, the young hacker gained access to key military and intelligence documents about CIA operations in Iraq and Afghanistan.

---

[24]The Democratic National Committee is the governing body of the Democratic Party, one of the two main political parties of the United States.

[25]The Central Intelligence Agency is the United States institution that ~~spies~~ gathers foreign intelligence to help the president in matters of national security.

Social engineering can be mitigated first and foremost by educating the users of your systems on the importance of checking the authenticity of emails and web pages before disclosing any private information. It is also important to enforce strict identity verification for every user in your systems when they change their password or update some other security setting. But these precautions are not enough: in more sophisticated attacks, the victim only needs to click a web link or to open an attached document for the hacker to *pwn* the system.

Software Vulnerabilities

Programmers know that parts of their code doesn't always work exactly as intended. As software becomes complex, the different situations it handles grows exponentially—and so does the risk for an unexpected situation to occur where a combination of inputs lead to an unwanted behavior.

These unwanted behaviors may cause the system to crash. They may cause secret information to be exposed. In the worst case, an intruder might be allowed to execute any piece of code. We call the sequence of inputs that leads to such unwanted behaviors a **vulnerability**. Let's now see some common types of vulnerabilities.

BROKEN ACCESS CONTROL This occurs when a system performs a potentially dangerous action without checking if the user has permission to perform it, for example when developers forget to add permission checks to their code or when a piece of software is misconfigured. In 2016, a tech company working with voter data left their database online without a properly configured password. As a result, private data from 154 million US voters was exposed. Read the manuals from all software you choose to use and configure them properly to restrict access.

SQL INJECTION It's the most common vulnerability. It enables a hacker to run any SQL[26] code in a database, which often allows attackers to arbitrarily read, write and delete data. Imagine that

---

[26] SQL is a database language for consulting, inserting and modifying data. We present it in our first book, *Computer Science Distilled*.

you're a school manager and a new student joined your school. The school clerk enters the name of the new student into a computer. The school's management software uses the name typed by the clerk to send an SQL query like this to its database:

```
INSERT INTO Students (name)
VALUES ('■');
```

In this example, the input ■ should be replaced by the software with the name that the clerk typed into the system. What would happen if the clerk tried to register the name below?

```
Robert'); DROP TABLE Students;--
```

If the school's software is vulnerable to SQL injections, it will blindly copy whatever input into the query. Here's the query that would now be executed by the system:

```
INSERT INTO Students (name)
VALUES('Robert'); DROP TABLE Students;--');
```

When inserting a new student record with this maliciously crafted name, there is a side-effect: an entire table gets deleted from the database. To defend against this kind of attack, check all your inputs and replace any character that can cause side-effects, such as quotation marks.[27]

SQL injection attacks are quite common. In 2012, hackers attacked several US government websites, including NASA, the FBI and the Pentagon. As a result, personal data from over a million employees and contractors became publicly available on the Internet.

Injection attacks are one of many types of vulnerabilities caused by bad handling of inputs. You must check not only the content, but also the *sizes* of external inputs you allow into your system.

---

[27] Besides the SQL injection, there are other types of injections where an input is run into a system causing unwanted consequences. For example, when copying user inputs into an HTML page, ensure the < and > characters are replaced, to prevent the injection of malicious tags.

BUFFER OVERFLOW Before programs can process any input, the input must be copied to an internal memory space called a **buffer**. If the input data is larger than the buffer and there are no checks in place, data will continue to be copied into the memory and *past the end of the buffer*. This means parts of the input end up in unintended locations of the memory. This is called a **buffer overflow**. It may cause the system to crash, or worse: if an attacker manages to write data in a specific location, the host computer might be tricked into executing parts of the input as code.

When hackers are given the opportunity to execute malicious code in a machine through a buffer overflow, they will often obtain full control over it. This type of vulnerability is difficult for hackers to find, yet it is common in major operating systems and consumer software. For instance, in 2015, one was found in Adobe Reader, a widespread application for opening PDF files. Before Adobe released a software update to fix the issue, hackers could craft a PDF file containing malicious code that would trigger a buffer overflow. If users opened the document on their computers, the malicious code would be covertly executed!

ZERO-DAYS Many companies offer large bounties for hackers who responsibly report security vulnerabilities. However, many black hat hackers and government spying agencies prefer not to disclose the vulnerabilities they find, since they might sell their details to other hackers or use them on high-profile targets. Vulnerabilities that aren't publicly known to exist and are used by a select group of hackers are called **zero-day** vulnerabilities. It's estimated that every widely used piece of software or operating system has several zero-days. This would mean that almost any computer can be hacked by government agencies and elite hacking groups.[28]

Exploits

Vulnerabilities are often discovered in mainstream software. After word about a new vulnerability is out, hackers are quick to code a generic attack sequence for susceptible systems. Such a piece of

---

[28]Because of this threat, the Russian Federal Guard service reportedly stopped using computers in 2012 for certain communications, favoring mechanical typewriters instead.

code is called an **exploit**. Depending on the vulnerability, an exploit can bring a vulnerable machine offline, expose private information, or worse: make the computer execute malicious code. If an exploit is made public, anyone can use it to hack into vulnerable systems with minimal effort.[29]

Every day, the number of known vulnerabilities grows, and there are elaborate tools that help hackers take advantage of them. For example, *Metasploit* is a program that automatically screens a system for known vulnerabilities and runs the relevant exploits. To do this, Metasploit consults a large, regularly updated database of vulnerabilities and their respective exploits. It can also scan computers over a network and probe each one for possible vulnerabilities.

Just as hackers can use these tools to find weaknesses in your systems, so can you! Organizations that develop and maintain these hacking tools believe in *offensive security*: making it easy to hack into known vulnerabilities so that people can also easily know where their systems are insecure and require attention.

ROOTKITS & KEYLOGGERS The bad code hackers try to execute on their victim's computer is called a **payload**. There are two main types of payloads. **Rootkits** allow the hacker to covertly access a shell in the host computer. **Keyloggers** record everything that's typed on the keyboard so that it can later be retrieved by the hacker. If the hacker manages to make their victims execute these malicious payloads, they will typically remain hidden and run in the background undetected, causing harm for a large period of time.

ANTIVIRUS SOFTWARE A so-called **antivirus** inspects all the data that is stored in a computer and the code that it executes. It tries to detect payloads and prevent them from being run or propagated further. Antivirus software providers constantly monitor the Internet and catalog any rootkit or keylogger they can find. However, hackers relentlessly mutate payloads in order to evade detection. At any given time, there are several strains of payloads that haven't yet been discovered by any antivirus provider. Antivirus software helps, but it doesn't defend against sophisticated attacks.

---

[29]An amateur who knows little about security and only cares to download and run exploits created by *real* hackers is called a script **kid**die, or **skid**.

Due to the pace at which exploits propagate, developers are expected to release updates fixing software vulnerabilities as fast as possible. Once there is an update fixing a vulnerability, it is said to have been **patched**. People using the vulnerable software should apply security updates as fast possible to avoid getting *pwned*.

Developers should always stay informed about the libraries they use to ensure they're not building on third-party code that has unpatched vulnerabilities. Likewise, system administrators should stay informed about the newest patches to the software they're running, especially for critical infrastructure such as web servers, mail servers and database servers.

There's a resource that can help us stay informed: the Common Vulnerabilities and Exposures (**CVE**) public list. As soon as a vulnerability becomes known, it is added to the CVE list and is assigned a number. If you check typical software update descriptions, you will often see patches to security vulnerabilities referenced by their CVE number. You can consult the CVE list to be aware of any known vulnerabilities in the software you're currently using.[30]

BOTNETS Some hackers have automated the process of scanning the Internet for vulnerable computers and running exploits to inject their rootkits. After years of running automated exploits, some hackers end up controlling an army of remote computers called a **botnet**. Experts estimate there are botnets operating today with hundreds of thousands of computers. Hackers often rent these botnets for others to use as a launchpad for further attacks. If you weren't cautious with your computer's security, it might secretly be part of someone's botnet!

FIREWALLS There's another type of software that can help protect computers from harmful exploits: the **firewall**. It blocks IP packets that aren't expected to be transiting in a network. For instance, if a computer isn't expected to be waiting for TCP connections initiated from the outside, a firewall can be installed to block all external IP packets that attempt to initiate a TCP connection. This makes it

---

[30]You can search the list at http://code.energy/cve.

much more difficult for a hacker to communicate with a malicious payload installed through an exploit.

BACKDOORS Vulnerabilities in computer systems aren't always there by accident. A vulnerability that was intentionally inserted into a system by a programmer or engineer is called a **backdoor**. Sometimes, law enforcement agencies or the military will request hardware manufacturers or software providers to include backdoors in their systems. Though the intent can be for them to be known only by good guys, black hat hackers can also discover and exploit them.

A backdoor can even exist in something as fundamental as an algorithm. It was uncovered on several occasions that the NSA pushed for the adoption of purposefully altered cryptographic standards that they were capable of breaking. In 2004, the NSA even bribed a lead software provider $10 million dollars to use such sabotaged algorithms by default. When it comes to selecting ciphers and other cryptographic tools for your own systems, do your own research and find those that are recommended by independent academic experts you trust.

Digital Warfare

Computer systems are essential to the functioning of a modern country. They control the communications of both the public and private sectors. They run power plants and the electrical grid. They're the backbone of banks and markets. Air traffic controllers and their radar systems rely on them. Railroad networks and their trains are also operated by computers.

It would be a catastrophe if an attacker could hack into all of these systems at once. Communication lines could be cut, bank accounts and markets wiped out, power plants shut down, radars blacked out, trains derailed... in short, it would be Armageddon.

We've already witnessed cyberattacks on high-profile military targets. In 2010, American and Israeli hackers used zero-day vulnerabilities to write a virus they named **Stuxnet**. It was programmed to infiltrate computers inside Iran's nuclear facilities. The virus spread slowly and eventually infected computers controlling uranium-enrichment centrifuges. It instructed the centrifuges to intermittently spin at different velocities, repeatedly straining them until they started to break. The virus also falsified instrument readings to evade detection.

Iranian intelligence eventually discovered the virus, but had they taken a few more months, they might have missed it: Stuxnet was programmed to ultimately delete itself, leaving little to no trace behind. Stuxnet is the most advanced case of digital warfare we know of, but it wasn't an isolated act. Many more clues suggest that digital warfare operations are currently ongoing between the hacking teams of different countries.

Armed forces of powerful nations invest heavily in Computer Network Exploitation (**CNE**): the training of hackers and development of exploits for spying and reconnaissance operations. They also invest in Computer Network Attack (**CNA**): the deployment of digital weapons that can sabotage enemy systems, for example destroying data or disabling communications.

An interesting case of CNA was carried out by the Israeli military in 2007. Israeli Air Force fighter jets flew deep into Syrian airspace *as if it were completely undefended* and destroyed suspected nuclear facilities. It later came to light that the Israelis had hacked computer systems of the Syrian Air Defense Force in order to falsify radar readings. This allowed the Israeli aircraft to conduct their operations meticulously and leave without taking a single shot from their adversaries.

For technologically advanced nations, there's an upside to the widespread presence of security vulnerabilities. Lives of their spies and soldiers on the ground are less at risk. Instead of spies risking their lives and taking years to infiltrate enemy headquarters physically, they can now directly hack into enemy computers and steal sensitive documents remotely. Instead of sending troops or launching ballistic missiles to destroy a nuclear facility, they can break into servers and run malicious software to destroy the facility from within.

At a smaller scale, private corporations also sometimes engage in digital warfare with each other by infiltrating their competitors and hunting for strategic documents such as financial reports or blueprints of secret new inventions. Inspired by the military, they deal with the threat of cyberattacks by training their employees to become hackers through so-called *red team vs blue team* exercises: the red team must *pwn* a given computer system, while the blue team tries to repel the attack. Some companies even hire professional hackers for the red team.

QUANTUM COMPUTING Cryptography and security are always evolving. Today, the military and intelligence services of powerful nations are investing heavily in the research and development of *quantum computers*. They could well become a reality this century, and the first nation to obtain one could potentially *pwn* the world. In microseconds, these computers will be able to solve problems that our current supercomputers can't even solve in a trillion years.

Once fully functional quantum computers are built, almost all cryptographic algorithms we use today will become insecure. However, brilliant minds are already working relentlessly on creating the ciphers of the future that will remain secure when the quantum computing revolution unfolds.

Defense Checklist

When initiating an attack on your systems, malicious hackers typically follow some of these steps:

1. Build a fake version of your service and send emails to your users asking them to type their passwords in.
2. Call your users claiming to be from tech support and make them reveal credentials or sensitive information.
3. Place covert SQL commands in all inputs handled by your system that are likely to be part of a database query.
4. Attempt privileged actions such as creating a new user without the proper permissions.
5. Probe for buffer overflows by sending very large chunks of data to every possible input that's handled by your system.
6. Build a script for interacting with your authentication software and to try to crack passwords via brute force.
7. Scan your network probing for known vulnerabilities.

Preparing your system to handle all these threats is the first step to improving the security of your systems.

Conclusion

Cryptography enables security in the digital world. It allows us to work with sensitive data even on insecure infrastructure. Digital security depends on three things: strong cryptographic tools, software vulnerability patching, and user awareness of social engineering threats.

We learned about the most important cryptographic tools. Symmetric ciphers are used for secretly transmitting and storing data. Asymmetric ciphers are used for digital signatures, digital certificates, and the establishment of shared secret keys over insecure connections. Hashing helps us guarantee and verify data integrity and handle secret passwords.

History teaches us the importance of staying up-to-date with advancements in cryptography, as the vast majority of cryptographic tools can end up broken one day. It also teaches us that hackers almost always attack systems by finding ways to bypass cryptographic defenses rather than breaking them. This can be done by exploiting software vulnerabilities or simply by manipulating humans into opening the gates. These techniques have become an essential part of modern warfare, where mission critical computer systems can be relentlessly attacked by enemy state-sponsored hackers.

This chapter was an introduction to cybersecurity, where we presented the basics we believe anyone in charge of potentially sensitive systems should know. If all developers were familiar with the concepts from this chapter, many of the destructive security breaches from the recent past could have been avoided.

Defending computer systems against sophisticated attacks isn't easy, and it can sometimes only be done by highly skilled security specialists. After all, a successful defense team must protect against *all* possible attack vectors. An attacker only needs to discover a single vulnerability in order to wreak havoc. Because of this, defense teams generally implement several layers of security measure. When this is done well, exploiting a single vulnerability is not enough for an attacker to break into a system.

We have seen that malicious hackers can go to great lengths to steal data. In some cases, a large data leak can even bankrupt a company or severely damage a government. But what makes large amounts of data so valuable? In the next chapter, we'll explore how to understand and navigate large amounts of data—legally obtained data, that is.

Reference

- The Code Book, by Singh
    - Get it at http://code.energy/singh
- Serious Cryptography, by Aumasson
    - Get it at http://code.energy/aumasson
- Ghost in the Wires, by Mitnick
    - Get it at http://code.energy/mitnick
- Hands on Hacking, by Hickey and Arcuri
    - Get it at http://code.energy/hickey

CHAPTER 4

Analysis

> The future of data analysis can involve great progress.
> Will it? That remains to us, to our willingness to take
> up the rocky road of real problems, in preference
> to the smooth road of unreal assumptions.
>
> —JOHN TUKEY

D ATA POWERS KNOWLEDGE. Whether you're conducting a survey to measure customer satisfaction or running the Large Hadron Collider to advance particle physics, you expect to learn something from the data you collect.

Data can easily be misunderstood or misinterpreted. Fortunately, **data analysis** is here to help us generate reliable knowledge. Different scientists have different approaches to data analysis, often depending on the nature of their research and the amount of data they have access to. This chapter proposes a data analysis workflow for programmers, divided in four stages: *collection*, *processing*, *exploration*, and *testing*. You'll learn to:

- 🌱 **Collect** data reliably and comprehensively,
- ✂️ **Process** it into a clean and robust dataset,
- 🔍 Kick off exploration by **summarizing** values,
- 🔭 Explore deeper through data **visualization**,
- 🧠 Draw conclusions by **testing** your intuitions.

Even the best of us will often overlook crucial steps in this sinuous process. We'll record inaccurate measurements, ignore important information, or draw incorrect conclusions. What's more, data analysis is iterative: at any stage, we may realize that an earlier step could be improved. It can quickly become a convoluted process.

To avoid creating a mess, we must be methodical. It's tedious, but rewarding. Rigorous data analysis helped Charles Darwin to

133

discover the origin of species, and may enable SpaceX to make life multiplanetary. Wield it on your most ambitious projects.

Intelligence

Imagine you own a small, struggling coffeehouse. In order to develop a profitable strategy, you must know your business. Which drinks do your customers prefer? How many coffees are sold per day? How much does an average customer spend? At what time do most customers come and go? Do your suppliers compare favorably to others? Did these metrics evolve over the past few months?

The answers to these questions are valuable, as they allow you to plan effectively and to define key performance indicators to gauge and track progress. To compile such essential knowledge, well-managed organizations analyze their data and create periodic reports. Workers and managers can then easily review progress and identify areas for improvement.

Many organizations do more than issue reports on their data—they track it in real time, such that the consequences of their actions can be monitored on virtual dashboards. Such processes support decision-making through learning and distributing information, and they form what people call **business intelligence**.

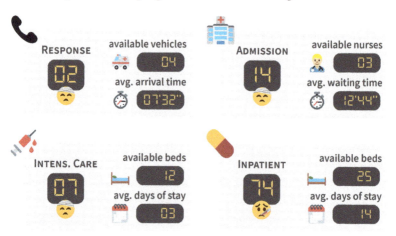

Figure 4.1 Hospital emergency room dashboard, tracking in real time the number of patients 😖 across different units.

Business intelligence isn't limited to commercial business. Consider a public hospital's emergency room where one can use a "business" intelligence dashboard to track the flow of patients (fig. 4.1). Then, for example, if there is an unusual spike in waiting times, hospital admission staff are quickly alerted and can address the situation before it escalates.

As a result of this intelligence, the hospital is also better prepared for crises. If a serious accident occurs nearby, the hospital will be able to immediately observe a drop in the number of available ambulances. Knowing what resources are at hand, the staff can quickly decide whether to call in reinforcements before the dispatched ambulances even return.

Business intelligence and other ventures in data analysis require you to collect, summarize, visualize, and learn from data. We will explore all of these topics. If your organization isn't focused on business intelligence and knowledge-management, lead by example. Study relevant data and share your findings in a compelling report or on a simple dashboard. You will create immense value.

4.1 Collection

Useful knowledge only emerges from relevant data. It can be difficult, when facing a colossal volume of irrelevant information, to identify the data that matters. Refine your search by predefining your goals. What information is related to these goals?

If your goal is to improve the menu of your coffeehouse, then the characteristics of both successful and failed products matter. Collect opinions from your baristas and your customers. Likewise, data on ingredients, pricing, and sales all relate to your goal. What if your goal is to improve patient care at a hospital? Look at which factors are considered to diagnose patients and track their recovery. Collect data on patients, diseases, and treatments.

Kinds of Data

Try to obtain the full picture when approaching your study. Capture information from all possible angles, so you will be less likely to overlook important details. If you're measuring temperatures, for example, it can be useful to know the time and place those measurements were made and if it was sunny, windy, foggy, or rainy. As programmers, we like to use the following categorization to check that we didn't neglect relevant data:

🔢	NUMERICAL	Score count, physical measurement...
🗄	CATEGORICAL	Olympic sport, movie genre, dog breed...
⏱	TEMPORAL	Date of birth, UTC−08:00 time...
🌐	GEOGRAPHICAL	Position, home address, border...
🍳	UNSTRUCTURED	Audio recording, email body, webcam footage, cooking recipe...

The first four kinds of data are said to be **structured**, as they are organized in a predefined manner. For instance, electric power is measured in Watts, every medal at the 1896 Olympics was awarded for one of nine possible sports, dates can be organized in a calendar, and international borders are defined along coordinates.

Computers are good at handling structured data. On the other hand, **unstructured** data is hard for them to digest. There are special methods for extracting structured data from unstructured data. For example, facial recognition software can take an unstructured video feed and output someone's identity as categorical data.

Getting Data

Many of our daily activities are facilitated by computers, therefore our behavior and actions often leave a digital footprint. Inspect computer systems to trace this data. Install your own sensors to collect even more, or change how your company operates. Additionally, you can often get useful data from third parties.

EXISTING DATA Hospital computers often monitor vital signs of patients, such as heart rate and body temperature. Restaurant computers record what was ordered at each table. What data do your computers manipulate? Scavenge *all* systems for copies of useful records. For example, explore the machine hosting the company's website and you will most likely find a log of all web visitors.

NEW DATA There is always interesting data going unrecorded. For instance, most restaurants don't record how happy customers feel after a meal. To remedy this, each bill can come with a slip for the customer to rate the service on a scale from one to ten. As long as you're not transgressing ethical boundaries, always look for ways to capture more data. If a restaurant's billing system isn't recording how long clients remain seated, change it.

Figure 4.2 Remember to show empathy when you're collecting data.

SENSORS We often think of sensors for studying natural phenomena; for example, climatologists need sensors for temperature, air pressure, humidity, and more. However, sensors can also be valuable for businesses: restaurants can use sound meters to track the ambient noise that their customers experience, and shopping malls often use presence sensors to record a daily visitor count. Moreover, web applications often use **virtual sensors** in order to track the behavior of users, such as the time they spend on individual pages.

EXTERNAL DATA You can use data that was collected by others. For instance, real estate brokers will consult third-party data for the price history of properties. Movie lovers can find data on most commercial films, and sport enthusiasts can find data pertaining to most professional matches. Governments typically provide census data, revealing important national socio-economic indicators. Use Google Dataset Search[1] to query thousands of data collections from companies, universities, and government agencies. You might find extra data that's relevant to your goals.

---

[1]Google Dataset Search: http://code.energy/google-data.

SCRAPING Oftentimes, relevant data from the Internet cannot be downloaded—it's only available on web pages. For instance, some websites compile reviews of bars and restaurants. If you need this data, write a script that visits those pages and copies the relevant chunks to your computer. This is called **web scraping**, and it's fairly common—there's even free software that automates the process.

PRIVACY Be careful not to collect personally identifying information about people without their explicit consent. It's simply unethical. Furthermore, do *not* trick people into accepting intrusive privacy policies, as some companies do with their lengthy terms and conditions that nobody ever reads.

Selection Bias

Imagine you own the restaurant collecting customer satisfaction slips. You're receiving more submissions than you can process, so you decide to only survey 10% of clients. If the staff selects who gets surveyed, they might prefer to pick customers in a good mood. As a result, data could indicate customers are more satisfied than what we would observe if *everyone* got surveyed.

This problem is called **selection bias**. It could also occur if you only give slips to clients who sit at specific tables. They might feel differently because they're seated in a noisy spot or have the sun in their faces. This could affect responses, and your data would still not reflect reality. Let's consider another example:

ARMORED ACE ♠ You're Wald, a mathematician during Wold War II. Enemy air defenses are taking their toll on the Navy, and you have mapped out all the shots that returning planes sustained. The engineers tell you they must limit weight, thus they can only add armor to one of three locations: the wings, the fuselage, or the engines. Which would you pick?

At first, it seems that adding armor to the fuselage or wings is best, as that's where most shots hit. However, the data is extremely biased: you only mapped shots from *returning* planes. You didn't map shots from planes that were lost! It turns out many crashes resulted from engine damage. The best way to save pilots is to add armor there.

Our biases are often hard to spot because they act on our intuition in ways we don't expect, and selection bias is no exception. Always ensure nothing affects *which* records are collected by selecting *at random*. And be aware that, like Wald, you sometimes simply can't collect unbiased data.

4.2 Processing

Collecting a lot of data is like filling up a warehouse with goods. It can be tempting to dump everything onto random shelves and become immediately distracted by the cool new stuff we're storing. However, the better organized the warehouse, the easier it will be to work. Organize your data as soon as it comes in.

Data Wrangling

The process of data collection typically yields myriad files: logs, SQL database dumps, spreadsheets, etc. These are called **raw sources**. The relevant chunks of information within these files have to be identified, extracted, and organized in a way that makes them easy to access. For example, extracting data from a web server access log can look like this:

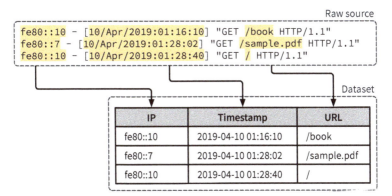

Figure 4.3 Extracting data from a web server access log.

Select only *relevant* data from the raw sources. Extract it and crunch it into new files using a format that computers can easily understand. We call these new files a **dataset**. Well constructed datasets can be directly analyzed without further organization. The process of transforming raw sources into a dataset is called **data wrangling**. Let's explore the steps involved.

TABULARIZATION Tables are the most common way to structure data. They're the default structure for data processing: most algorithms work best on tabular data. Each table stores records of events or objects of the same kind. The first step of data wrangling is to divide all relevant data into tables.

In tables, every record becomes a row. The different things we know about these records become columns. In the context of data analysis, columns are also referred to as *variables*. Figure 4.3 shows a raw text source being copied into a table with three variables: IP, Timestamp, and URL.

Usually, tabular data is saved in CSV[2] format. CSV files can be readily imported into virtually any programming environment. If your tabular data is stored in a relational database,[3] it's often worth the effort to convert the data into CSV files. This ensures you have one table per data entity, making analysis much simpler: there's no need to resolve relationships across different tables in order to interpret the data.

NORMALIZATION Always check that cells in the same column are uniform. When there are several ways to express something, you must **normalize** the data. For instance, if a column contains temperatures, choose either Fahrenheit or Celsius[4] and convert other values. Three examples of normalization are illustrated on the next page.

---

[2]Comma-Separated Values (CSV) is the simplest format for storing tabular data. It is plain text where commas and new lines delimit cells and rows.

[3]Relational database systems such as *MySQL* and *PostgreSQL* use formats that allow splitting and storing data across multiple tables. Programmers do this in order to eliminate information repetition. Our first book, *Computer Science Distilled*, explains the advantages and disadvantages of relational databases.

[4]Scientists typically normalize data to the metric system so that their numbers are easier to manipulate and compare with data from around the world.

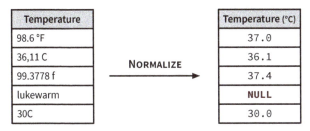

Figure 4.4 Normalizing temperature. Be consistent in the number of decimal digits and the use of commas and periods. Remove extra F, C, or ° characters, and discard or re-express values that aren't numbers.

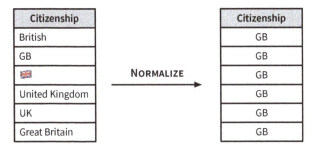

Figure 4.5 Normalizing citizenship records. Be ready to handle unexpected cases, especially with old records. Should people from the Soviet Union be considered Russians? What about Yugoslavians?

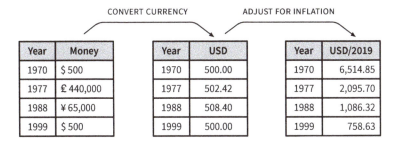

Figure 4.6 Normalizing figures from different currencies and years. Because of inflation, one dollar in 1970 had the same purchasing power as six dollars in 1988. On top of that, some currencies don't even exist anymore, such as the Italian lira! We need historical exchange and inflation rates to normalize such numbers.

Normalization can also involve splitting a column into two or more. Imagine that a museum's database of paintings has a "dimensions" column containing text describing canvas sizes. It would make sense to split this into height and width columns, each containing well formatted numbers in a uniform measurement unit:

Name	Dimensions
No. 5, 1948	8 ft × 4 ft
Las Meninas	318 x 276 cm
The Scream	91 cm, 73.5 cm
Monalisa	30¼ by 21⅞ in

→

Name	H (cm)	W (cm)
No.5, 1948	244	122
Las Meninas	318	276
The Scream	91	74
Monalisa	77	53

Figure 4.7 Normalizing painting dimensions.

CLEANSING Always check that your values are of the expected type, and that they are reasonable. Clear cells that contain absurd data. This is called **data cleansing**.

DROP THE BEAT ♥ As the manager of a hospital's business intelligence systems, you compile a report with the heart rate measurements of many patients. As you inspect the data, you come across some astonishing values, such as 819 beats per minute. What should you do about them?

Time	Patient	Rate (bpm)
07:00	472	61
07:01	677	78
07:03	780	819
07:04	472	180

A heart rate can never be negative. A quick Internet search informs us the highest heart rate ever recorded was about 600 beats per minute. Records outside the range $(0, 660)$ can be safely dropped.[5] The cell that reads 819 should be set to NULL, or removed entirely.

Be very careful that zeros are *never* used instead of NULL when a cell lacks data. In the temperature records example (fig. 4.4),

---

[5]Most humans have a resting heart rate of 40–100 beats per minute. Nonetheless, depending on what we're analyzing the data for, it's sometimes good to leave some room for extraordinary but authentic data. Here, a 10% margin above the record high was chosen arbitrarily.

it would have been wrong to normalize "lukewarm" to a freezing 0.0 degrees Celsius! Unfortunately, this careless practice is all too common. For instance, a lot of software outputs the coordinates (0°, 0°) when it can't obtain a location.[6] No matter the type of data you have collected, check your zeros—are they accurate numerical records, or should they be NULL?

DUPLICATES Ensure your tables have no duplicates: each row must record something unique. Let's say a table stores the titles, release years, and genres of different movies. It should contain only one row for each movie. If two rows read "Metropolis, 1927, Sci-Fi", delete one of them.

Duplicates are harder to spot when data isn't yet normalized. If a record has the genre Sci-Fi, and its duplicate, Science Fiction, a simple search won't find the problem. Duplicate names with spelling mistakes or alternate spellings often survive undetected. Always normalize and cleanse your data, and carefully inspect similar rows to destroy duplicates. If you use a database management system, find which built-in tools and functions can help you do this.

Data Anonymization

Have the utmost respect for data that details people's lives. Financial records, health care data, and private messages are only a few examples of immensely sensitive information that can never become public. In many organizations, everybody keeps a copy of the sensitive data they work with. A catastrophic data leak is just a hack away! Handle and store private data with extreme care.

To mitigate risks, data should be transformed so that the amount of personally identifiable information is reduced. This is called **data anonymization**. Many countries already have laws that mandate anonymization of data in certain cases.[7]

---

[6]In fact, according to many uncleaned data sources, that empty spot in the middle of the Atlantic ocean is one of the busiest places on Earth. Nerds even gave it a name: "Null Island".

[7]For an example, see Europe's General Data Protection Regulation (GDPR).

DROPPING Discard data that only serves to identify people. For example, first and last names, social security and tax identification numbers, phone numbers, and email addresses will almost never have any statistical relevance. Data without connections to demographics, organization goals, and behavioral patterns can be promptly dropped.

BLURRING Some personally identifiable data shouldn't be dropped. For instance, age is important demographic information that often explains behavior—keep it. *Exact* dates of birth, however, can be used to find people and endanger anonymity. Store the year of birth alone: it preserves a sufficient indication of age, and it's not personally identifiable. This process of sacrificing precision in favor of anonymity is called **data blurring**.

Think of simple ways to decrease the precision of sensitive data. Suppose you work for a business that needs to keep track of customer spending. Will keeping records down to the penny help understand their behavior? Drop the cents to make records more anonymous. This also applies to their home address: the zip code is likely sufficient to target people in a specific area. Blur out the unnecessary precision.

RE-IDENTIFICATION Even carefully anonymized data can sometimes be "de-anonymized". This process is called **data re-identification**: if you know enough about someone, you can filter the anonymized records and identify which one belongs to that person.

Consider an anonymized dataset from a hospital. If you know someone's age, sex, duration of stay, and type of illness, you can probably match his or her exact record in the anonymized dataset. Data anonymization is a deterrent, not a solution. Give anonymized data the same level of protection and secrecy as your raw sources.

Reproducibility

It can be tempting to get the data processing phase over with as soon as possible, without scripting and documenting every step. Such quick, dirty, and poorly documented jobs are said to have been done **ad hoc**. In general, ad hoc data processing is very bad practice.

More often than not, new versions of the raw data will emerge. Sometimes, we simply receive a fresh data dump with additional records. If transformations were made ad hoc, it is difficult and time-consuming to repeat them on the new data. Furthermore, it is difficult to check if errors occurred during ad hoc data transformations: at any given stage, we can't compare the state of the dataset to previous stages. Moreover, an identified error can be very difficult to revert.

In order to avoid these issues, experienced data scientists ensure every transformation can be easily repeated. This is called **reproducibility**. You could achieve a basic level of reproducibility by documenting all the ad hoc transformations you perform in a log, but all the operations would still have to be carried out manually.

Best practice is to write a program that performs all data transformation steps in a pipeline. This way, when data sources change, we can replay the transformations simply by running the program on the new raw sources. When working in a team, every member can inspect this program, which makes it easier to find bugs. Then, if a bug is found, it can be fixed in the program, and a new corrected dataset can be generated by running the upgraded program again.

Crucially, never modify your raw sources directly: newly wrangled and anonymized data should be written to new files. Your raw sources hold the truth if ever you suspect there was an error and you need to roll back operations. If the raw sources contain sensitive information, don't forget to ensure their access is restricted.

Now that your dataset is squeaky clean, you're ready for the next stage: *exploration*. This is where the real fun begins. In the coming sections, you will discover the foundations of Exploratory Data Analysis, or **EDA**. You will learn to *summarize* and *visualize* your data. As you *see* the data, your intuition will develop. This intuition can generate questions about the underlying phenomena that shaped the data. These questions can, in turn, guide you deeper in your analysis: it is always easier to find something when you know what you are looking for.

4.3   Summarizing

We can summarize many important characteristics of a dataset in a few key numbers. This provides us with a quick idea of what the data says without having to inspect individual records. Let's see some of the most useful summarizing numbers:

Count

Nicknamed "the n", it's the number of individual records you have. For instance, if a health care table describes the hospitalization of two dozen patients, then $n = 24$.

Averages

An average is the "central" or "typical" value of a group. There are several types of averages. The most ubiquitous is the **mean**: sum all values and divide by the count. Means are good averages, but they aren't perfect. Let's see why:

BITCOIN BUBBLE 🅱   Five friends claim to be blockchain experts and convince you to buy \$100 in cryptocurrency. Each friend tells you how much they think the value of your wallet will change in dollars within a week depending on the coin you buy. You are considering Bitcoin, Ether, and Dogecoin. Which of those should you get?

Expert	BTC	ETH	DOGE
Adam	8	NULL	7
Gavin	6	2	7
Roger	NULL	4	7
Sergey	NULL	3	−1
Vitalik	7	21	−2

Which is better, BTC's $(8, 6, 7)$ or ETH's $(2, 4, 3, 21)$? It's hard to compare groups of numbers. To make it easier, we can summarize each group into a single number. Let's try with the mean:

	Earning prediction (\$)					
Coin	Adam	Gavin	Roger	Sergey	Vitalik	Mean
BTC	8	6	·	·	7	7.0
ETH	·	2	4	3	21	7.5
DOGE	7	7	7	−1	−2	3.6

Ether's higher mean hints that it has the best earning potential. However, note that Ether's mean is heavily influenced by a single extremely high prediction. Maybe Bitcoin is a better bet, despite its lower mean.

In contrast, the **median** is an average that stays unaffected by the extreme values of the group. To obtain the median, sort the values in numerical order and pick the one in the middle. For Dogecoin, we find $(-2, -1, \underline{7}, 7, 7)$. If the number of elements is even, no single central value exists, like for Ether: $(2, \underline{3}, \underline{4}, 21)$. The median is then the mean of the two central elements. In any case, the median will always indicate the center of the group: it's greater than half the values and less than the other half.

	Earning prediction ($)					
Coin	Adam	Gavin	Roger	Sergey	Vitalik	Median
BTC	8	6	·	·	7	7.0
ETH	·	2	4	3	21	3.5
DOGE	7	7	7	−1	−2	7.0

The median isn't perfect either. Notice how Bitcoin and Dogecoin exhibit the *same* median of seven dollars, although the experts offer very different predictions: 100% agree Bitcoin will earn around seven dollars, whereas 40% say Dogecoin will register losses!

While the mean considers all the numbers of a group, it's very sensitive to extreme values. The median isn't affected by extremes, but it ignores all values other than the central one. Together, mean and median are complementary ways to average numbers.[8]

Variability

Whether we use the mean or the median, we cannot know how precisely it represents its group of numbers. For example, $(9, 10, 11)$ and $(0, 10, 20)$ both average to 10, even though the values of the former are much closer to 10.

---

[8]There are more types of averages, such as the **harmonic mean**, which will be used in the next chapter. Some averages are ideal for rates of growth, others, for travel speeds. To learn more, head to http://code.energy/average.

The **standard deviation** of a group of values indicates how far they tend to be from the mean. When the standard deviation is larger, the numbers are more spread out. Most programming lan guages have built-in functions that compute standard deviation.[9] Let's see how it can be used:

INTELLIGENT INVESTMENT 👵 Your grandma wants to invest in tech! Since she plans on paying the membership fees of her bridge club with the returns, she needs you to deter-mine which one of the three stocks she is considering can provide the most stable yearly income. Based on their five year history of returns (in %), how can you compare the volatilities of these three stocks?

Year	AAPL	GOOG	MSFT
2014	40.0	-2.4	27.2
2015	-2.8	46.6	22.2
2016	12.2	1.7	14.7
2017	48.2	32.9	40.2
2018	-5.1	-0.8	20.2

For each stock, you can calculate the standard deviation of its yearly returns, as this is a good indication of the volatility.

	Total return (%)					
Stock	2014	2015	2016	2017	2018	Std Dev.
AAPL	40.0	−2.8	12.2	48.2	−5.1	21.8
GOOG	−2.4	46.6	1.7	32.9	−0.8	20.2
MSFT	27.2	22.2	14.7	40.2	20.2	8.6

Among these stocks, Apple and Google displayed similar volatility, whereas Microsoft yielded more stable returns year-to-year.

You can use standard deviation every time you calculate a mean: it can be a measure of a bowman's precision, the temper-ature variations in a town, or income inequality in a population. Remember to use it to describe how well the mean summarizes a group of values.

---

[9]**Variance** is another common measure of variability. The variance is simply the standard deviation squared.

Five-Number Summary

Suppose you are considering a few cities in which to spend your summer, and for each city you found a database containing the peak temperature of every single day of the year 2018. How can you estimate the number of days of enjoyable weather each city will offer? For starters, the median of daily peak temperatures is informative: it divides the days such that half were cooler than the median, and half were warmer. We can repeat this process and divide the halves into quarters:

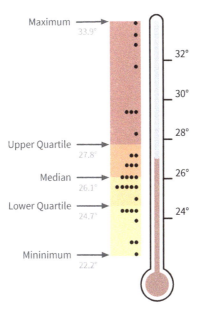

Figure 4.8 Daily peak temperatures (°C) in Los Angeles (July 2018). Each point represents one day. Since $n = 31$, each quarter of the data comprises eight points.

After the median divides the ordered data points into halves, the **upper quartile** divides the *top* half into quarters and the **lower quartile** divides the *bottom* half into quarters. The upper and lower quartiles—along with the mean, minimum, and maximum—constitute the **five-number summary**. Many modern programming languages have libraries for easily outputting these numbers. Here are the summaries for daily peak temperatures of a few cities in the entire year of 2018 ($n = 365$):

Table 4.5 Five-number summaries of peak temperatures.

City	Min	Lower Quartile	Median	Upper Quartile	Max
Rio de Janeiro	20.1	26.8	29.9	32.8	39.1
Los Angeles	13.9	19.4	22.2	25.0	34.4
Honolulu	23.9	27.8	29.4	30.6	33.3
Minneapolis	−17.1	0.9	10.6	26.7	37.8

These summaries illustrate interesting factors to consider when you're choosing where to spend the summer: even if Minneapolis is freezing a quarter of the year, the warmest 91 days are warmer than in Los Angeles!

OUTLIERS We sometimes stumble upon abnormally high or low values, which don't seem to be reasonable when considering the other values in the column. These values typically indicate extreme events that are markedly different in nature. It pays to single out these values and study them carefully. In order to identify these values systematically, scientists define normality boundaries. Values outside the boundaries, if any, are marked as **outliers**.

There are many methods to define a normality boundary. For example, we often start by subtracting the lower quartile from the upper quartile. This difference is called the **interquartile range**, or **IQR**, and values further than $1.5 \times$ IQR from its closest quartile are then considered outliers.

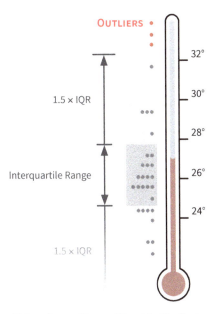

Figure 4.9 Identifying the outliers of fig. 4.8. We find an interquartile range of 3.1°, so 1.5 × IQR ≈ 4.5°. The higher boundary is therefore 32.3°, and the lower boundary is 20.2°.

There are no lower outliers in the temperature measurements of July 2018 in Los Angeles: all the values are above the lower boundary (fig. 4.9). On the other hand, there's a cluster of four warm days, three of which are outliers with highs of 32.4°, 33.3°, and 33.9°.

Those were different in nature indeed: a record-breaking heat wave struck southern California from July 6 to July 9, 2018. On the 7th, the high temperatures enabled a huge wildfire to engulf many streets of Santa Barbara. Over two thousand people had to be evacuated from the area, and thermometers inside the UCLA campus recorded their warmest temperatures ever.

Categorical Summary

Records of categorical data contain labels rather than numbers, so we can't directly summarize them with an average, a standard deviation, or a five-number summary. However, we *can* count them.

We typically summarize categorical data by counting the number of times each category occurs. When category counts are expressed as a percentage of the total count n, we get the frequency at which each category was recorded. For instance, a table with each Olympic medal and its winning nation at the 1896 summer games can be summarized by counting the most frequent countries:

Country	Count	Frequency
Greece	46	38%
United States	20	16%
Germany	13	11%
France	11	9%
Great Britain	7	6%
Others	25	20%

Correlation Matrix

When it rains, roads become more slippery and visibility decreases; therefore, car insurance companies expect more traffic accidents. Imagine you are such an insurance company, and you collected a dataset with three columns such that each row contains a date, the amount of rainfall at that date, and the corresponding number of traffic accidents. You would expect to see the values in the two last columns increase and decrease together: the more it rains, the more accidents happen.

When two such columns vary together, we say the columns are correlated. We can express the strength of the phenomenon with a number called the **correlation coefficient**, or "correlation" for short.[10] A correlation coefficient of 0 means the values do not vary together *at all*. A correlation coefficient of 1 indicates the two columns vary together perfectly.

In practice, the correlation coefficient is rarely equal to exactly 0 or exactly 1. To quickly search for relationships between columns of our tables, we calculate the correlation values for every pair of

---

[10] Several methods to measure correlation exist. Each yields a slightly different coefficient. Here, we use the Pearson correlation coefficient, aka Pearson's r.

columns in the table. The results can be compiled in a **correlation matrix**, which summarizes how much columns vary together.

For example, suppose you work for the City of Los Angeles, and you constructed a table where each row is a day, and columns represent the daily peak temperature, the day's average wind speed, rain volume, the number of traffic accidents, and the number of assaults registered by the police department. Building a correlation matrix reveals the relationships among these variables:

Table 4.7 Correlations in daily events (Los Angeles, 2018, $n = 365$).

	🌬️	☂️	🌡️	💥	🔪
wind 🌬️					
rainfall ☂️	0.21				
temperature 🌡️	−0.18	−0.19			
accidents 💥	0.05	0.19	0.18		
assaults 🔪	−0.03	−0.11	0.28	0.07	

From top left to bottom right, there is a diagonal of ones: columns perfectly correlate with themselves. Furthermore, the top-right half of the matrix is symmetrical to the bottom-left half: the correlation between 🌬️ and 💥 is equal to that between 💥 and 🌬️. All these grayed out values offer no additional information and are generally removed from the correlation matrix for clarity and concision.

Notice that some of the columns have negative correlation coefficients, such as 🌡️ and ☂️. Negative correlation values indicate that columns vary together but in *opposite* directions: as more rain is registered, lower peak temperatures are recorded.

When correlation values are close to zero, we say they are virtually uncorrelated. For example, accidents don't seem affected by wind speeds. Conversely, the strongest correlation we have is between 🔪 and 🌡️. The data seems to suggest that criminals tend to be more aggressive when the weather is warmer.

Such a correlation matrix helps us explore how columns are related to each other. When two variables correlate, investigate the causes in the real world, you might make interesting discoveries.

CAUSALITY There is a trap. When we find a correlation between two phenomena, we are often quick to assume that one caused the other. This is not automatically the case. For example, shopping malls typically register a high correlation between their sales of sunglasses and of ice-cream. Does this imply that wearing sunglasses makes you crave ice-cream? Or that eating ice-cream causes your eyes to be more sensitive? No. Always keep in mind that *correlation does not imply causation.*

Figure 4.10 "Correlation", courtesy of http://xkcd.com.

TRANSFORMATIONS Columns often have to be transformed for correlations to be found. For example, accidents due to skidding in your city might correlate poorly with rainfall or vehicle speeds, but correlate strongly with the amount of rainfall *times* the speed limit *squared*. It can become tricky to find the transformations that reveal such correlations. If the correlation coefficient of two columns or their transformations is close to zero, this does not necessarily mean that those two variables are not related to each other.

Summarizing numbers simplifies and reduces the amount of information we have to consider. Much of the nuance, however, remains out of our reach, and it can be difficult to find a path forward. Capturing more of the data by using shapes and colors is the next step of exploration. A picture is worth a thousand numbers!

4.4 Visualization

The mean, standard deviation, and five-number summary provide a helpful but simplistic overview of a dataset's story. To uncover more clues, we must resort to our visual pattern recognition instincts. Graphing and plotting allow us to see the data, explore its patterns and nuances, and reveal anomalies caused either by extraordinary events or—more commonly—by simple processing mistakes.

Box Plots

There is a graphic representation of the five-number summary, and it's called the **box plot**. The upper and lower quartiles are drawn as the upper and lower sides of a box, and a horizontal line divides the box at the median. Whiskers protrude over and under the box to reach for the maximum and minimum *non-outlier* values, and outliers are often added as individual points. Let's construct a box plot for the July 2018 temperatures in Los Angeles:

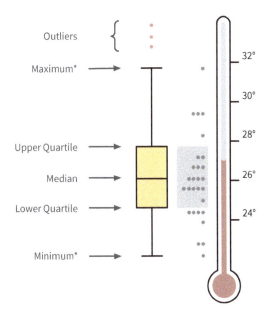

Figure 4.11 Constructing from fig. 4.8 a box plot of daily peak temperatures in Los Angeles in July 2018 ($n = 31$ days).   *ignoring outliers

Notice that increasing the amount of data to the entire year affects the box plot (Figure 4.12). Then, check out how box plots can be used to compare different cities on a single chart (Figure 4.13).

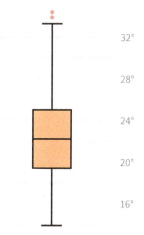

Figure 4.12 Box plot of daily peak temperatures in Los Angeles in *all* of 2018 ($n = 365$). Only two outliers remain because the entire set of 365 data points has a different interquartile range and normality boundaries than the set for July only.

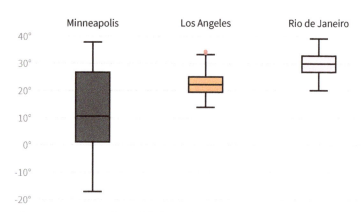

Figure 4.13 Box plots of daily peak temperatures in 2018. Minneapolis and Rio de Janeiro do not display outliers.

While a table makes it easy to read the values of a five-number summary, the box plot makes it easier to compare the distributions described by different five-number summaries.

Histograms

The five-number summary describes the sub-ranges covered by groups of numbers, and you've learned to obtain it in two steps: you (a) divide data points into groups of equal size, and (b) observe what ranges they cover. Conversely, a **histogram** depicts precisely *where within the range* data points are concentrated, and it is prepared through the opposite process:

   (a) Split the range into intervals of equal size, called **bins**,

   (b) Observe how many data points each bin contains.

Finally, we can **(c)** plot each bin as a bar whose height represents the number of data points it contains. The next figure shows the construction of a histogram with 10 bins, but we could have used any number. The figures thereafter demonstrate how varying the number of bins changes that plot and how histograms can help us compare temperatures in different cities.

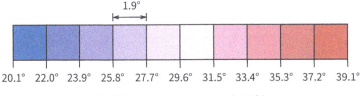

(a) Split the temperature range in 10 bins.

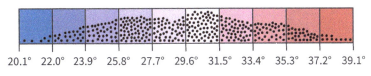

(b) Place 365 daily peak temperatures into their bins.

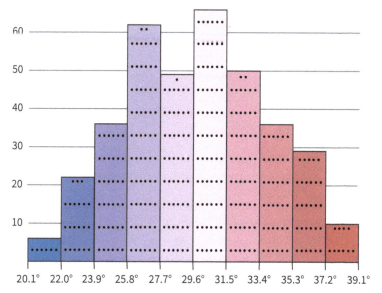

(c) Stretch each bin so its height represents the number of dots it contains.

Figure 4.14   Creating the histogram of daily peak temperatures in Rio de Janeiro, which ranged from 21.1°C to 39.1°C in 2018. Note that in typical histograms, all bins share the same color.

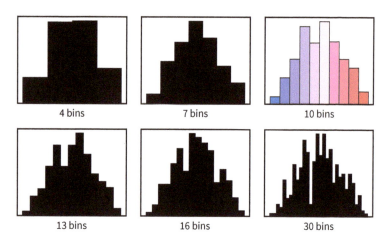

Figure 4.15   Six histograms of the same dataset. More bins give a more precise depiction of the distribution. However, too many bins make your histogram look bumpy and unclear.

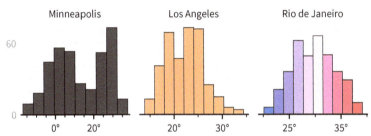

Figure 4.16 Histograms of peak temperatures for different cities in 2018. We can immediately see that Minneapolis is the perfect town if you dislike mild temperatures and enjoy extreme ones—whether they're burning hot or freezing cold!

CUMULATIVE HISTOGRAMS There's a different way to do histograms. Instead of each bin's height only representing the number of data points it contains, we can also add the number from previous bins. Therefore, bins only get taller as we move to the right. Here's how to obtain such a **cumulative histogram** from a regular histogram:

(a) Scale down fig. 4.14c.

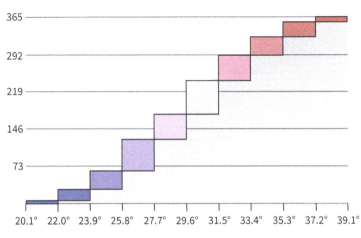

(b) Stack each bin on top of the previous.

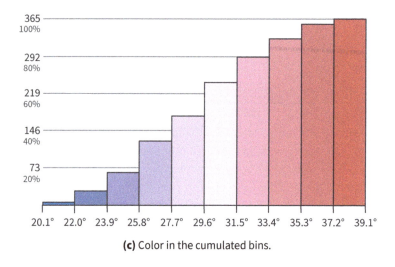

(c) Color in the cumulated bins.

Figure 4.17 Creating a cumulative histogram.

Notice that the bin ending at 33.4°C has a height of 292. This tells us that 292 days, or 80% of the year, were cooler than 33.4°C. Let's now compare our four cities with 10-bin cumulative histograms:

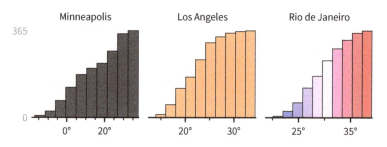

Figure 4.18 Cumulative histograms of peak temperatures (2018).

When observing any graph, always inspect its scales. The temperatures in Minneapolis and Rio de Janeiro might seem rather similar in fig. 4.18, but these plots have very different scales on the horizontal axis. If we plot one histogram over the other, the differences between the cities become apparent:

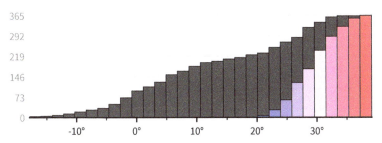

Figure 4.19 Comparing peak temperature cumulative histograms of Minneapolis (gray) and Rio de Janeiro (colored). The bins were carefully defined on the same temperature intervals for both cities. Since the ranges don't match, Rio de Janeiro gets some empty bins!

Scatter Plots

So far, we've seen plots that explore *one* variable—or column of data. The **scatter plot** explores how *two* variables relate to each other. In this plot, each data record is one dot. A dot's position on the vertical axis represents the record's value in one column. The dot's position on the horizontal axis represents the record's value in the other column. The next figure shows how to construct a scatter plot from the data points in fig. 4.11:

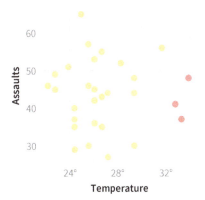

Date	Temp.	Assaults
Jul 05	26.7°	55
Jul 06	33.3°	37
Jul 07	33.9°	48
Jul 08	31.7°	56
Jul 09	32.8°	41
⋮		

Figure 4.20 Los Angeles number of recorded assaults versus daily peak temperatures in July 2018. Temperature outliers in red.

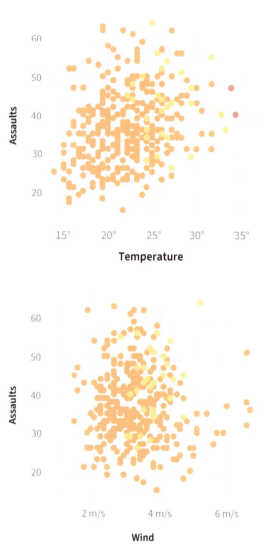

Figure 4.21 Number of assaults versus daily peak temperatures, and then the average wind speed for the rest of 2018.

From the correlation matrix tab 4.7 on page 153, we know assaults and wind aren't correlated, but that there is a correlation of 0.28 between assaults and temperatures. Can you see from the plot that warmer days *tend* to have more assaults?

It will be easier to spot a correlation with temperature if we have data that covers a greater range of temperatures. Let's try the daily recorded number of criminal offenses in Minneapolis:

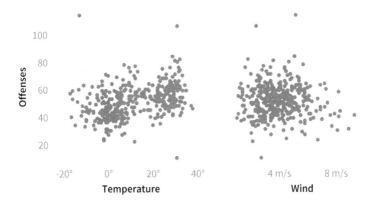

Figure 4.22 Number of offenses versus daily peak temperature and average wind speed in Minneapolis for every day of 2018.

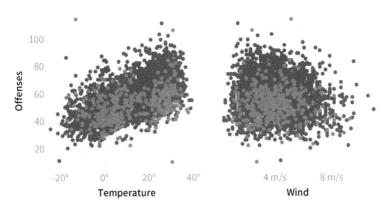

Figure 4.23 Number of offenses recorded in Minneapolis from 2010 to 2018. Each plot has more than 3000 points, therefore many overlap and the visualization is difficult to interpret.

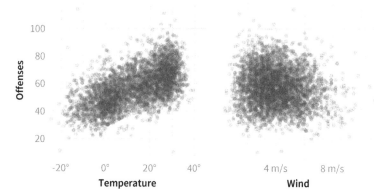

Figure 4.24 Minneapolis number of recorded offenses from 2010 to 2018 at 20% opacity. Darker shades of gray form in the areas with a higher concentration of points. The plot on the left has a correlation coefficient of 0.58: warmer days tend to suffer more crimes. There is no apparent pattern between wind and crime, and the data points shown on the right yield a −0.11 correlation.

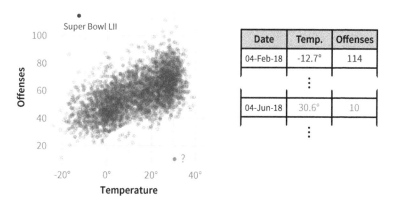

Date	Temp.	Offenses
04-Feb-18	-12.7°	114
⋮		
04-Jun-18	30.6°	10
⋮		

Figure 4.25 Pay close attention to outliers: the lonely dots far from all the others. Find out to which rows these dots correspond. The cold day with many offenses is 4 February 2018, when the Super Bowl took place in Minneapolis! The warm day with few offenses has no obvious explanation, so it could very well be an issue with the police department's data collection system.

Time Series

If your data points all have an associated time stamp, you can plot them in chronological order and trace a line connecting consecutive ones. This type of graph is called a **time series**. It can reveal interesting relationships and patterns between your data and time. Here's a time series of daily peak temperatures in Los Angeles in July 2018, using the same data as fig. 4.11:

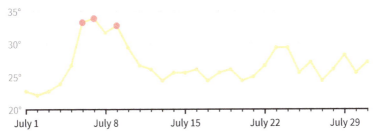

Figure 4.26   July 2018 Los Angeles peak temperatures.

When a time series has many points packed too close together, variations between consecutive points can add a lot of jitter to the plot. Observe what happens if the same plot is made with every single day of the year, using the same data as fig. 4.12:

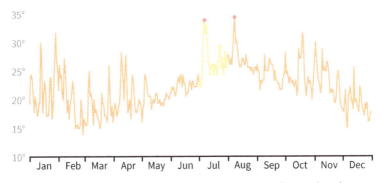

Figure 4.27   Los Angeles peak temperatures over all months of 2018.

In such cases, we can smooth the plot to make it easier to read. One common technique is called the **moving average**: each data point is replaced by the mean of *itself and a few preceding points*. The number of preceding points used is called the **window size**. Let's see how this looks like.

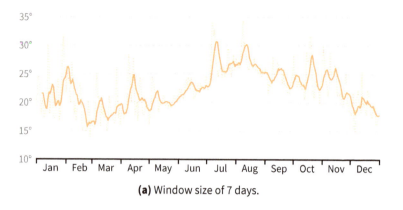

(a) Window size of 7 days.

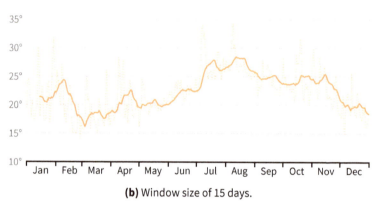

(b) Window size of 15 days.

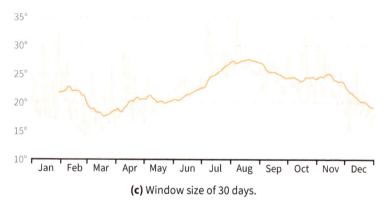

(c) Window size of 30 days.

Figure 4.28 Moving averages of daily peak temperatures over the year 2018 in Los Angeles at different window sizes. Increasing the window size makes the moving average of our time series smoother every time.

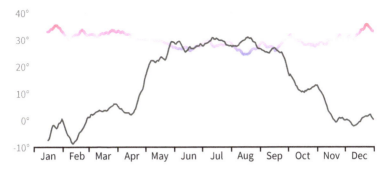

Figure 4.29 Comparing the 15-day moving averages of peak temperature time series of Minneapolis (gray) and Rio de Janeiro (colored).

We already knew from the box plots (fig. 4.13) and the histograms (fig. 4.19) that peak temperatures in Rio de Janeiro and Minneapolis have very different distributions. Now, we can clearly see that they are almost the same from June to August, when it's summer in Minneapolis and winter in Rio!

Many other events are also influenced by the time of year. For instance, ice-cream sales are higher in the summer, and occurrences of respiratory illness are higher in the winter. Once you plot your data in a time series, seasonal patterns become very easy to spot.

In general, time plots are useful when we need to understand how a variable grows or shrinks over time. For example, the price of storing digital data has reduced, fueling the data science revolution. To fully realize how dramatic the change has been, let's plot the cost of data storage over time:

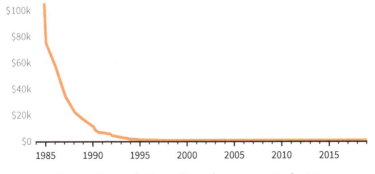

Figure 4.30 Inflation-adjusted storage cost of 1 GB.

In 1985, it cost over $100,000 (in 2019 dollars) to store one giga-byte of data. In 2018, it cost less than 3¢. As the scales of these prices are several orders of magnitude apart, the line in the plot flattens out after 1995 and it's difficult to discern what's happening from that point onward.

LOGARITHMIC SCALES There is a helpful trick to view data across such orders of magnitude: trade the common **linear scale** for a **logarithmic scale**. A linear scale is defined such that each tick is equal to the previous *plus* some number. In fig. 4.30 on the previous page, each tick on the vertical axis was equal to the previous *plus* $20k. On the other hand, a logarithmic scale is defined such that each tick is equal to the previous *times* some number. The number 10 is often chosen, as it makes the ticks display nice round numbers:

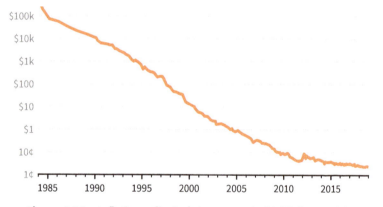

Figure 4.31   Inflation-adjusted storage cost of 1 GB *(log scale)*.

Observe how storage prices from 1995 to 2018 no longer resemble a flat line. It is now possible to precisely read the storage prices from each year. From 1985 to 2010, the price per GB became roughly ten times cheaper every 5 years, except between 1995 and 2000, where prices decreased by a whopping factor of almost 100!

In 2011, terrible floods struck Thailand, claiming the lives of 815 people and affecting millions more. Many factories were badly damaged, disrupting global supply chains for hard disk drives throughout 2012. This tragic event explains the very visible spike in prices on fig. 4.31.

Maps

When you have geographical data, show it on a map. If, for example, you know the daily peak temperatures for every county in the USA, you can create a heat map:

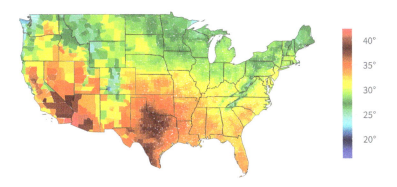

Figure 4.32 Mean maximum daily temperature in July 2018, revealing cool areas around the Rocky and Appalachian mountain ranges.

Mapping is not limited to geographical data. For instance, when aerodynamics engineers obtain temperature values for every point in space of an airflow, they will map it in three dimensions:

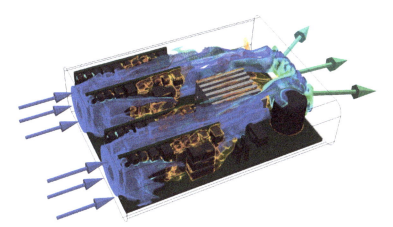

Figure 4.33 Fan-generated wind cooling down an electronic circuit board. The air at the vent (right) is slightly warmer than at the fans (left).

4.5 Testing

As we explore data and identify patterns, we often devise theories to explain what we observe, and many of those turn out to be misguided or wrong. As the famous cosmologist Carl Sagan said during his last ever interview:

> *"Science is more than a body of knowledge. It is a way of thinking; a way of skeptically interrogating the universe with a fine understanding of human fallibility."*

It can feel deeply unnatural to question one's own assumptions, and subsequently, it is challenging to explain patterns conclusively. Thankfully, scientists value skepticism and developed tools to help.

Hypotheses

In order to address a question or intuition without drawing inaccurate conclusions, start by framing it properly. Express it as a **hypothesis**: a statement that can be supported or rejected by data you can collect. You will have to test the hypothesis, so do *not* assume it's true or false yet. Make your hypothesis simple and objective, so that it's easier to test.

> TASTE BUD TEST 🍧   Your coffeehouse in Minneapolis was losing its vegan customers. Ten days ago, you decided to update the menu and offer green tea and coconut-milk ice-cream. You did so without any research, based on the following intuitions:
>
> 🍵 *Vegan customers craved green tea on yoga days,*
> 🍨 *Customers didn't like the old ice-cream selection.*
>
> Now that the new menu is up and running, you wish to conduct a study to determine whether changing the menu was a good decision. Can you express each of your intuitions as a hypothesis? Try to formulate one that relates to your goals and that you can easily test.

For 'Intuition 🍵', it's hard to find an objective measure of *craving*. However, one of the goals of your business should be to sell your products, so you can express the hypothesis as follows: *Vegan customers **buy** green tea on yoga days*. Testing this hypothesis could help you understand if your decision is likely to regain the loyalty of vegan customers. However, it requires some work: you must conduct a survey with personal questions to determine which customers are vegan yogis.

'Intuition 🤢' is tricky to test, as surveying long-time customers can expose you to selection bias: you can only survey those who return, who are more likely to have enjoyed the old menu. However, this intuition is intimately related to your business goal of selling products, so a hypothesis could be:

📊 *Ice-cream sales are higher with the new menu.*

This hypothesis doesn't give you much insight as to *why* you are achieving or not your ice-cream goals, but at least it is easily testable: your accounting system has likely been collecting sales data before and after the menu change. You have all the data you need already! Using an average, let's summarize and compare the last 100 days of the old menu with the first 10 days of the new one:

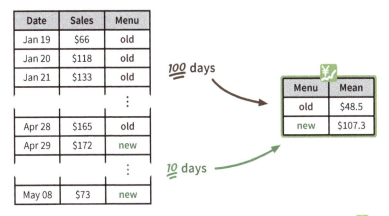

Figure 4.34 Summarizing daily sales in order to test 'Hypothesis 📊'.

This data agrees with the hypothesis: sales were higher when the new menu was used. Is this evidence sufficient to confirm our hypothesis that the new menu would increase ice-cream sales?

No. *No* conclusions can be drawn by comparing averages over this small dataset. Many other factors may have affected the data. Changes in customer behavior could stem from other changes made to your coffeehouse, such as the table layout. They could result from factors outside of your control, such as the weather:

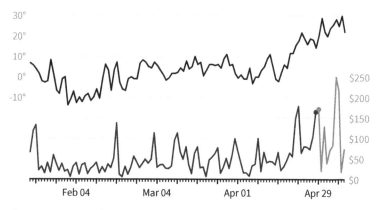

Figure 4.35   Daily peak temperatures and ice-cream sales at your coffeehouse in Minneapolis. Temperatures are shown on top in black (left scale), ice-cream sales are shown under in color (right scale).

Regardless of your menu, customers will surely eat more ice-cream on a hot day than during a blizzard! Maybe higher temperatures caused the increase in sales, not the new menu. Maybe you were lucky. And if you can't be sure of what caused the change in sales, how can you know if the result of the hypothesis test reflects the truth? In the next sections, we'll delve into the methods scientists developed to address this issue with diligence.

Experiments

Good researchers develop procedures to reduce the uncertainties around their results. A scientific procedure to test a hypothesis is called an **experiment**. Hypotheses can only be properly tested via well-designed experiments.

The first step of experiment design is to identify the variables you need to measure and the data you must subsequently collect.

For 'Hypothesis ', these variables are *sales* and *menu*. We already have them as columns in fig. 4.34.

There are always other variables that affect those you wish to study. We call them **extraneous variables**, and watch out: they can potentially lead you toward wrong conclusions. Try to collect data on extraneous variables if your records don't already include them.

If you observe fig. 4.35 closely, you will notice peaks in sales seem higher when the weather is warmer. The sales are fairly irregular, but we can notice a peak in sales every seven days. Maybe people eat more ice-cream on weekends! We already identified two extraneous variables: *temperature* and *day of the week*.

When you're exploring the data, keep searching for clues to identify different extraneous variables. When you find them, make sure your records are updated accordingly:

Date	Sales	Menu	Day	Temp.
Jan 19	$66	old	Fri	6.7°
Jan 20	$118	old	Sat	5.6°
Jan 21	$133	old	Sun	3.9°
⋮				
Apr 28	$165	old	Sat	14.4°
Apr 29	$172	new	Sun	20.6°
⋮				
May 08	$73	new	Tue	22.2°

Figure 4.36 Collecting data on factors that may influence sales.

In a well-designed experiment, the hypothesis is tested using records where the variance of extraneous variables is minimized. However, this may severely restrict the number of usable records. For instance, if we only consider the same day of the week with a similar peak temperature, only two data records remain:

Date	Sales	Menu	Day	Temp
Apr 22	$179	old	Sun	17.8°
Apr 29	$172	new	Sun	20.6°

Figure 4.37   Comparing sales in similar conditions.

Sales were lower with the new menu in this experiment. The data does not support 'Hypothesis 💹', therefore we're a bit closer to rejecting it. But can we reject it?

No. Even when designing an experiment in a controlled environment, we can never control *everything*. There are always other factors that affect the data, some of which are difficult to identify. Could you possibly have known that your sales were boosted both by a group of competitive eaters visiting the area and by an unusual number of homes with malfunctioning freezers? Conversely, could you possibly have known that an unexpected surge of pollen allergies kept people home, reducing your potential sales? The world is too complex for you to identify *all* extraneous variables, no matter how hard you try.

NOISE   At some scale, the complexity of our universe will always yield random fluctuations independent of any extraneous variables we can find. Such random unexplained fluctuations are colloquially called **noise**. When too few data points are available, it's difficult to know which fluctuations are noise and which are not, and the truth gets blurred. Ultimately, the more data we have that supports a hypothesis, the closer we get to confirming it. Conversely, the more data we have that disagrees with the hypothesis, the closer we get to rejecting it. Unfortunately, in fig. 4.37 there are only two data points, and that's insufficient to confirm or reject the hypothesis. We need more data.

Since it decreases uncertainty, one might be tempted to keep collecting more data forever. Let's try to determine *how much* data is enough to be confident that the hypothesis test result reflects the truth.

P-Values

Since it's always possible to be unlucky and obtain data that supports a false hypothesis, statisticians developed methods to estimate *how unlikely* it is that this occurred. This kind of method is called a **statistical hypothesis test**:

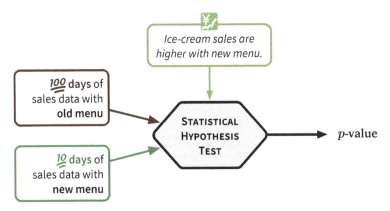

Figure 4.38   Statistical hypothesis test in action.

The probability that we were unlucky is called the **p-value**. The smaller the p-value, the closer we are to confirming the hypothesis. If the hypothesis is true, then collecting more data will tend to decrease the p-value.

There are many different types of hypothesis tests, each best suited for a specific scenario. For the p-value to be meaningful, do your research and make sure you pick one that corresponds to your data and hypothesis.[11] They all work in a similar way: you input experimental data, and they output a p-value for the hypothesis you're testing.

A probability is always a number between 0 and 1, and the p-value is no exception. Obtaining $p = 0.2$ means there's a 20% chance that your data supports a wrong hypothesis out of bad luck. If you're uncomfortable with that risk, collect more data. Run the test again, and if your hypothesis is correct, the p-value should

---

[11]For an overview of common hypothesis tests and how to use each test, see http://code.energy/hypothesis-test.

decrease. Now, will this finally be enough to confirm or reject the hypothesis with absolute certainty?

Nope. A p-value is never exactly 0 or 1. In other words, never claim a 0% or 100% chance that a hypothesis is false. Furthermore, be very careful in interpreting these probabilities because the result of a hypothesis test can only be as reliable as the data itself. If your data suffers from selection bias, then your p-value is irrelevant. Hypothesis tests do not substitute controlled experiments, they merely complement them.

STATISTICAL SIGNIFICANCE Even though the p-value can never be zero, there comes a moment when we must be able to draw conclusions. Usually, we define a maximum acceptable p-value that our hypothesis test should yield for it to be considered *probably* true. This threshold is called the **significance level**. When a p-value is below it, we can say there is **statistically significant** evidence supporting our hypothesis. Scientists typically work with significance levels between 0.05% and 5%.

Drawing conclusions from data without statistical significance is a common mistake. In many cases, we cannot possibly obtain enough data to produce statistically significant evidence supporting our hypotheses, and therefore we have to base our decisions on certain assumptions. It is important to recognize the limitations of our knowledge, and be ready for our assumptions to be proven wrong.

Figure 4.39 "Boyfriend", courtesy of http://xkcd.com.

Confidence Intervals

If we could try the new menu for an unlimited number of days, the mean daily sales would represent its true performance. Can we be confident that the mean daily sales of $107.3 we obtained with our experiment is equal to that truth? In other words, what p-value would we get by testing the following hypothesis?

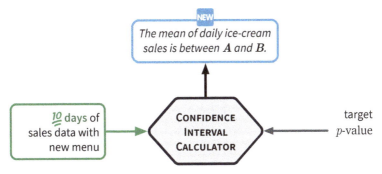 *The mean of daily ice-cream sales is $107.3.*

It is nearly impossible to obtain *exactly* $107.3 of mean sales as we keep on collecting data, therefore the chance that we do *not* get $107.3 is almost 100%. In other words, the p-value would be almost 1, which is far from the near-zero significance levels we want! In order to obtain a lower p-value, we must tolerate values close to $107.3. For example, we can test if the mean is between $A = \$97.3$ and $B = \$117.3$. The hypothesis then becomes:

The mean of daily ice-cream sales is between $97.3 and $117.3.

As we make the gap between A and B larger, the p-value gets smaller. When the gap is set such that the p-value is equal to our chosen significance level, we call (A, B) the **confidence interval**. Typically, we input our data and the significance level we are targeting into a function called a confidence interval calculator, which then outputs (A, B). There are different confidence interval calculators to choose from depending on the nature of your data and of the hypothesis. However, they all work in a similar way:

NEW
The mean of daily ice-cream sales is between A and B.

10 days of sales data with new menu → CONFIDENCE INTERVAL CALCULATOR ← target p-value

Figure 4.40 Finding the confidence interval.

Confidence interval calculators often ask for a **confidence level** instead of a significance level. The confidence level is equal to one *minus* the significance level. In other words, a confidence level of 95% is the same as a significance level of 5%; and conversely a confidence level of 99% is equivalent to a significance level of 1%.

Conclusion

Data analysis is a process you must follow diligently in order to draw convincing conclusions. To ensure the integrity of your results, channel your data through every step of the pipeline:

Save yourself headaches and do *not* skip steps or change their order. If the exploration phase reveals you have insufficient data to test your assumptions, make sure all phases are carried out thoroughly and repeated in order: collection, processing, exploration, and only then testing.

COLLECT When starting out, your primary focus is to gather and stockpile data of every possible type and from every possible source. As you scrape existing data or create mechanisms to capture new data, your main worry is to steer clear of any selection bias.

PROCESS Once the data is collected, make it easy for a computer to understand. During this phase, be a *wrangling* perfectionist: make sure every aspect of your dataset is organized and that only clean, valid, and consistent data remains. Moreover, you have the grave responsibility of *anonymizing* every last bit of sensitive data.

EXPLORE Once it is clean, *summarize* and *visualize* your dataset. Compare different groups of values, observe how they are distributed across their ranges, and plot them over time. When you detect abnormal properties, investigate the causes. Explore how your data reflects the intricacies of the real world.

TEST Finally, how do the insights you gained from exploration relate to your goals? Inspect the tables and plots that could affect decision-making. Formulate hypotheses and test if your data confirms them with statistical significance.

Abiding by these principles empowers you to make decisions based on evidence rather than intuition only. Yet, the best is still to come. By transforming your data a bit more, you can feed it to algorithms that will provide complex information about the future that human intelligence alone could never guess. Are you ready?

Reference

- The Data Science Design Manual, by Skiena

    - Get it at http://code.energy/skiena

- Everything is Obvious, by Watts

    - Get it at http://code.energy/watts

- Naked Statistics, by Wheelan

    - Get it at http://code.energy/wheelan

CHAPTER 5

Learning

> The question of whether computers can think is like the question of whether submarines can swim.
>
> —EDSGER DIJKSTRA

PREDICTIONS INFORM DECISION-MAKING. Many hundreds of years ago, ancient Mayans observed crops and astronomical patterns to predict yield and decide the best moment to plant their corn. Today, North American farmers can make more precise decisions thanks to advanced weather forecasting.

One way to predict the future is to look at the past, as often the best predictor of future outcomes can be found in past patterns. It's intuitive: if you notice a bar gets full most nights there's an NFL game, you start believing it will be busy the next NFL night.

Machine learning is using computers to crunch data on past events, find patterns, and unleash their predictive powers. This technology is everywhere. When you buy car insurance or get a loan, companies record your data. Over time, banks learn to predict who's likely to default their debts, and insurers guess who might crash their cars. This chapter shows you how they go about it. You will learn to:

- Turn collected data into **features**,
- Train a machine and **evaluate** it,
- **Validate** its predictions methodically,
- **Fine-tune** its gears for better results.

Without computers, we would need to spend a lot of time and energy and consult top experts to make predictions. With computers, we can automate them at scale. For example, banks can approve loans automatically, saving on personnel costs while serving customers faster. In health care, machines can automatically screen high-risk patients in order to deliver preventive care and save more lives.

Models

In the field of machine learning, an algorithm that makes predictions is called a **model**. Many different types of models exist, each making use of different math tricks. Some of these tricks are quite advanced, but don't worry: we're not diving into *how* models work. Instead, we'll learn how to *use* models.

Imagine you're a real estate agent in the town of Sweetwater, and you want to predict the price that three apartments will sell for. You first gather some clues, such as their distance to the city center, their age, and their area. You can organize them in a table X, where each column is a type of clue, known as a **feature**, and each row corresponds to one apartment sale. You can then append a column y_{pred} for your predicted prices:

X			y_{pred}
Distance	Age	Area	Pred. Price
0.4 km	4 yr	114 m^2	?
2.4 km	10 yr	68 m^2	?
3.4 km	16 yr	40 m^2	?

Figure 5.1 Apartments for sale in Sweetwater.

Filling in the column y_{pred} is no easy task. On its own, the features table X does not provide any reference price points. If the apartments were in Tokyo or Timbuktu, the prices would surely be different! In order to make decent predictions, we need examples to learn from. Let's add to the table apartments that were already sold in Sweetwater, labeled with their true sale price y, and call these records the **labeled dataset**.

Distance	Age	Area	Pred. Price	True Price
0.4 km	4 yr	114 m²	?	
2.1 km	8 yr	120 m²		$840,000
10.6 km	9 yr	91 m²		$540,000
0.5 km	3 yr	90 m²		$745,000
3.5 km	26 yr	35 m²		$185,000
2.4 km	10 yr	68 m²	?	
3.4 km	16 yr	40 m²	?	

X (Distance, Age, Area) — y_{pred} (Pred. Price) — y (True Price)

LABELED DATASET

Figure 5.2 Apartments for sale and sold apartments in Sweetwater.

From this table, you might start to think intuitively. The price of the 114 m² apartment is probably closer to $1,000,000 than $100,000. If you collect many more labeled examples, you can use a predictive model to help you out.

You don't need to code any model yourself to get started, as open-source machine learning libraries are available for most programming languages. Once a library is installed, its models can be imported into your code and promptly put to use.

TRAINING Before you can use a model to make predictions, you have to make it learn. The specific syntax depends on the programming language and on the library you are using, but it always comes down to calling a *training* function that takes as arguments the *X* and *y* tables of the labeled dataset. As they describe the same list of events, these tables must contain the same number of rows. As the model trains, it adjusts its internal cogs to find a math

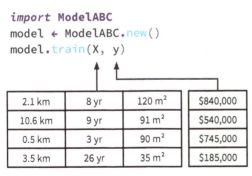

```
import ModelABC
model ← ModelABC.new()
model.train(X, y)
```

2.1 km	8 yr	120 m²	$840,000
10.6 km	9 yr	91 m²	$540,000
0.5 km	3 yr	90 m²	$745,000
3.5 km	26 yr	35 m²	$185,000

formula that approximates the values of *y* from the rows of *X*. Typically, *X* and *y* require a huge number of examples for the model to make good approximations. Depending on the application, this number could be in the thousands, millions, or billions.

PREDICTING Once the model is trained, we can start predicting. If we now take the rows of X for which y is unknown, we can use a *predicting* function to make the estimations y_{pred}. This output is the model's best guess for the values of y that will be later observed in real life. The predictions in this example are probably very unreliable.

```
y_pred ← model.predict(X)
```

$1,332,182	0.4 km	4 yr	114 m^2
$23,958	2.4 km	10 yr	68 m^2
$348,296	3.4 km	16 yr	40 m^2

In order to make better predictions, we need to train the model with way more than four labeled examples. Furthermore, this model only takes into account three features. Let's see how more data can be included in order to train more powerful models.

Figure 5.3 "Thanks to machine learning algorithms, the robot apocalypse was short-lived." Courtesy of http://smbc-comics.com.

5.1 Features

Data collection and processing must be performed carefully when the data will be used for machine learning. Before we even start worrying about training a model, we have to ensure we understand how the data we will feed it must look like. Imagine, for example, that you work for a hospital; and for logistical purposes, you want to predict how long each incoming patient will stay. If you start looking around for data, you will find hundreds of different tables in different formats.

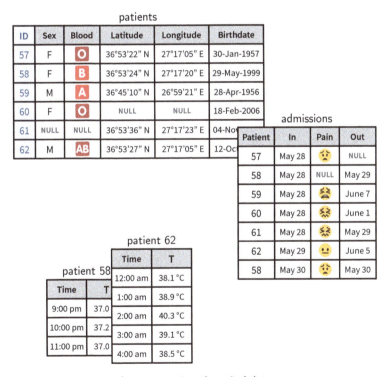

Figure 5.4 Raw hospital data.

Machines aren't intelligent yet, so we cannot simply throw data at them and expect them to train themselves and start predicting. We must digest the data into well structured X and y tables that models can work with. Let's see how it's done.

Adapting Data

The first step in building X and y from our dataset is to check we have the right kind of data. Most predictive algorithms work only with 🔢 **NUMERICAL DATA**. Let's see how to process other kinds of data so they can also be included as features.

🗂 **CATEGORICAL DATA** We say categorical data is **encoded** into numerical form. The encoding method will depend on whether your data is *binary*, *ordinal* or *nominal*. Let's see what this means:

Encoding *binary* data. It comes in two categories, therefore one category is expressed as 0 and the other as 1. Here, the raw data indicates the biological sex[1] of a patient.

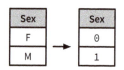

Encoding *ordinal* data. The categories are ordered, so we assign them numbers accordingly. For instance, if an emergency room admission form asks patients to select one of four emoji to describe their pain, it can be expressed with a number from 1 to 4.

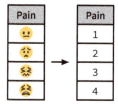

Encoding *nominal* data. When the categories of our column have no intrinsic order, we typically encode the column into several binary features: one for each category. This technique is called **one-hot** encoding. This example shows how it is used to express a patient's blood group in four features. Since a patient can only have *one* blood group, the encoded record must have one cell containing 1, and all other cells containing 0s.

Blood		A	B	AB	O
A	→	1	0	0	0
B		0	1	0	0
AB		0	0	1	0
O		0	0	0	1

---

[1]Up to 2% of us are born intersex, for instance with XXY chromosomes. A binary encoding may be used if predictions don't directly affect individual patients, for example if hospitalization times are estimated for internal logistical purposes.

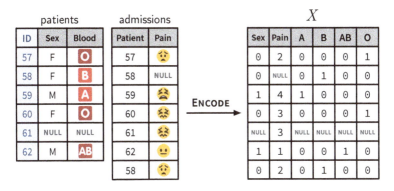

Figure 5.5 Getting features from different types of categorical data.

⏱ **TEMPORAL DATA** The most straightforward way to include date or time records is to extract their numerical parts: a date can be split into three separate features for year, month and day; and a time can be split into hours, minutes and seconds.

However, this is rarely helpful for a predictive algorithm. For instance, whether a patient is born in April or November should not affect their recovery time. On the other hand, whether they are twenty or sixty years old matters. Hence if you have the date of birth and the admission date, you can **construct** a new feature by calculating their age in years. If you are trying to predict how long they will stay in the hospital, you do the same for y: the length of stay is the number of days between admission and discharge.

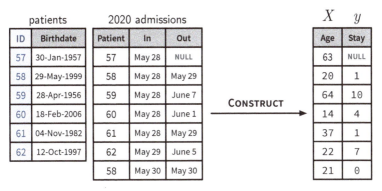

Figure 5.6 Getting features from temporal data.

One other way to construct a feature is to convert and encode temporal data as categorical data. For example, if hospitalizations due to intoxication are more frequent at night or on weekends, this could have an impact on y. You can make this information available in X as binary data. A lot of hidden information can be brought to light this way, such as the availability of open drugstores, the season of the year, or the occurrence of a holiday. Create

Date	Time		Wknd	Night
May 28	2:56 am		0	1
May 28	4:32 pm	→	0	0
May 29	11:05 pm		0	1
May 30	8:40 pm		1	1

features for the chronological and seasonal patterns that are likely related to what you want to predict.

🌐 **GEOGRAPHICAL DATA** Geographical data is often represented by numbers in coordinates of latitude and longitude. On their own, these numbers only indicate how far north and east a place is. The numbers may be separated into different numerical features, but just as for temporal data, these features generally don't help much.

To construct meaningful features from geographical data, think about how the locations you have relate to what you want to predict. It is often useful to calculate distances: if you want to predict the prices of apartments, you can construct features for their distances to the city center, to the nearest beach, or to the nearest school, supermarket and hospital.

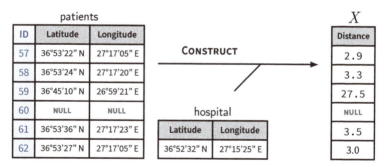

Figure 5.7 By converting patient addresses to geographical coordinates, their distance to the hospital may be constructed.

Numerical coordinates can be transformed into categorical data as well, such as the town, neighborhood, or zip code. Some of this categorical data can even allow you to add more information as features, such as matching indexes for income and criminality levels.

⚡ **UNSTRUCTURED DATA** It is estimated around 80% of the world's digital data is unstructured, and thus cannot be encoded as rows and columns but rather as individual files. Constructing features from unstructured data is difficult. In order to obtain numerical data from unstructured data, we must find what quantifiable aspects of it are relevant to our project.

Imagine, for example, that a set of patient records contain CT scans of their lungs. A useful number that physicians could obtain from the images is the area of the lungs of each patient.

The most common form of unstructured data is text. What quantifiable aspect of a text file could we be interested in? The total word count is a simple, popular one. Another prevalent feature is the occurrence of specific words. For instance, the fact that a medical report contains the words "tumor" or "cancer" can be encoded as binary categorical data. Or, if we take the number of occurrences of a key word and divide it by the total word count, we obtain the *frequency* at which it appears.[2]

Guessing which useful features could be hidden in unstructured data is easier when you can consult experts who collect and analyze it routinely. If you ask physicians what exactly they look for when they inspect medical reports or CT scans, they might give you interesting ideas to build relevant features.

Combining Data

Your raw data will often come in different shapes and sizes, and sometimes features can't be encoded without prior processing. Furthermore, some data points don't have much meaning on their own, but we can combine them with others. Let's see how to do this.

AGGREGATES If we have some information that comes as a collection of numbers for each record in X or y, we often can't encode every number as a feature. For example, if we're monitoring patient body temperatures several times per day, our dataset will contain many values for each patient's temperature. The summarizing tools from last chapter (sec. 4.3) can help transform this data into features:

---

[2]The **Bag-of-Words** is the most used method to create features from word frequencies. See http://code.energy/bag-of-words for more.

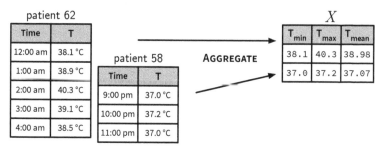

Figure 5.8 Constructing features by aggregating data.

When attempting to predict future performance, aggregations are commonly used on historical data—past performance is often a good indicator of future performance. For example, if you are predicting whether a team will win the NFL, construct features from the five-number summary of the team's score over the past years.

SCORES We can express an attribute of interest in a single number, even when the information related to the attribute comes from different variables. A **score** is a number generated by a math formula to represent a specific attribute. For example, the *body-mass index* is often used in health care, and is calculated from a patient's height in meters and weight in kilograms:

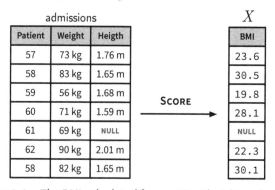

Figure 5.9 The BMI calculated from patient height and weight.

Well-designed scores encapsulate the knowledge of how multiple factors interact and contribute to a meaningful attribute. Calculating a score and adding it to X makes that knowledge accessible to the model. For instance, if you're trying to predict if people will develop diabetes and you have people's height and weight, include the BMI score as a feature. Obesity is a risk factor for diabetes, and its best obtainable measure is often the BMI.

In social sciences, the *human development index* (HDI) scores a country's development from its literacy rate, mean life expectancy, and gross domestic product (GDP) per capita. In finance, the FICO credit score describes a person's creditworthiness, given their net debt and payment history.

When there is no well-established score for a given metric, you can create your own. Suppose you're trying to predict the future sales price of apartments, and you believe the perceived safety of the building is a good indicator. You can construct your own "safety score" that combines many factors: the number of crimes registered in the neighborhood, the building's distance to a police station, and whether it has a doorman or a video-surveillance system.

After creating new features, revisit some of the data exploration techniques from Chapter 4. Build summaries and plots for the new features. This helps you check if the features were crafted correctly. Also, a feature's correlation coefficient with y can sometimes provide a preview of its predictive power.

Missing Values

Typically, the requirement for data to be *numerical* in X is strict: most predictive algorithms can't even handle NULL cells. When the value of a feature is unavailable for some records, we must get rid of those empty cells. There are several ways to do it.

DROPPING The simplest method is to remove from X all the rows that contain one or more NULL cells:

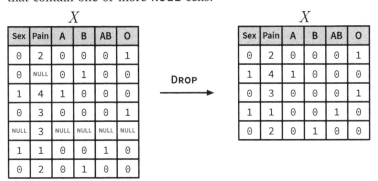

Figure 5.10 Dropping incomplete rows from X.

Dropping is a good approach when few rows are affected. However, decreasing the amount of X data for training generally decreases the performance of a predictive model, and deleting too many rows will limit its predictive power. Moreover, dropping rows doesn't only mean you have less data for training: it also means that you will drop the opportunity to make predictions for any important event with missing data.

Sometimes, we have a *column* where most of the values are missing. In such cases, dropping that feature from X is often a better option as it allows you to save many rows.

There is another way you can deal with missing data: filling NULL cells with a value you deem reasonable. This process is called **imputation**, and the three most commonly used fillers are the *most frequent*, the *average*, and the *new label*.

MOST FREQUENT If many values are repeated in a column, the most frequent such value is used in all NULL cells in that column. This is especially useful to resolve missing values in categorical data.

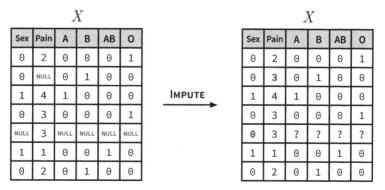

Figure 5.11 Imputations for binary and ordinal encodings such as biological sex and pain may be resolved directly in X. However, the one-hot encoding for blood type cannot be resolved this way since all of its columns contain mostly zeros.

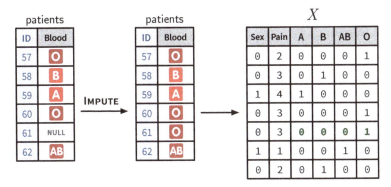

Figure 5.12 Nominal data must be imputed *before* one-hot encoding. This way, one of the imputed cells will be a **1**.

Notice that this operation must be performed *before* the one-hot encoding to ensure that each one-hot encoded row contains a cell displaying **1**. This is how we avoided filling the question marks in fig. 5.11 entirely with zeros.

AVERAGING Following this method, the **NULL** cells are filled with the average value of other cells in the column:

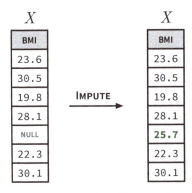

Figure 5.13 Imputing cells with the column's mean.

Typically, the mean or the median is used. Be careful with this strategy: it won't work with categorical features. For instance, if you try it with binary data, the empty cells could be filled with decimal values instead of ones and zeros.

NEW LABEL This strategy only works for categorical variables. When NULL cells are frequent in a categorical column, we can create a new label, and assign it to all cells with missing values.

> TEST TO TREAT 🦠 Your hospital is struggling with a novel coronavirus pandemic, and you must estimate how likely incoming patients are of needing a respirator. You test the patients for the virus and create a categorical feature where each is labeled 'negative' or 'positive'. There aren't enough tests for everyone, so priority is given to patients who display symptoms such as fever and coughing. In the end, only half the patients have been tested, 60% of whom turn out positive. How should you impute the NULL cells of untested patients?

Dropping the rows for untested patients is not an option, as it would cut out half of the records and render the model useless to predict, for example, the total number of respirators needed in the future. Using the *most frequent* value is problematic: most tests turned out positive, but tests were not administered at random, so the results don't necessarily generalize well to asymptomatic patients. This is a form of selection bias (sec. 4.1): patients without symptoms are less likely to have the virus than those with symptoms, so defaulting them to 'positive' would be a mistake!

Therefore, you have two options: ask the hospital to test a small sample of asymptomatic patients and generalize that result, or simply create a *new label* for untested patients. The former will allow you to keep a binary encoding for the feature, whereas the latter will require a one-hot encoding for the three final labels ('negative', 'positive', and 'untested').

Dropping records, selecting the most frequent values, calculating averages, and creating new labels are the simplest and most common methods of dealing with missing values. Scientists are actively researching new and more effective ways of imputing large datasets. In general, imputation is effective if missing data appears at random. If there's an underlying reason for some cells to be NULL, these strategies can hinder more than they help.

Data Leakage

When we're building X and y from past events, we might accidentally include in X information that only exists once y is observed. This is called **data leakage**. If this happens, the model will be trained to predict the future from future data, which is pointless.

As you add features into X, think about the information that will be available when you make predictions. Inspect X and ensure it looks exactly like the data your model will have to evaluate y_{pred}. Let's try this in practice:

> BUSY BEDS 🏥 You are in charge of a hospital's business intelligence system. The day following the admission of each patient, you are asked to predict how long they will stay hospitalized. You are given access to the following information about past patients: age, sex, BMI, blood type, vital signs, and total cost of stay. How can you choose which data to include as columns of your dataset?

The first step is to check when and how this information was collected. For example, let's assume age (🌡) and sex (⚥) are collected during admission, and blood type (🩸) shortly thereafter. However, height (📏) and weight (⚖), to obtain the BMI, typically come after a couple of days. Measurements of vital signs such as heart rate (❤), blood pressure (🎈), and body temperature (🌡) are made all along the patient's stay. Finally, cost of stay (💵) can only be calculated after the patient is discharged:

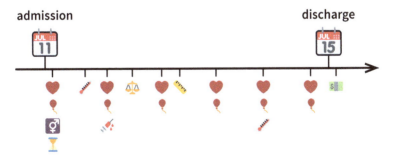

Figure 5.14 Time line of observations for a typical patient.

The length of stay y is observed at discharge. We can already see that including ▓▓ in the feature table X of labeled examples would be pointless, as it would amount to predicting the past! To determine precisely what data cannot influence X, let's add on the time line the moment y is observed, and when we would want the model to estimate y_{pred}.

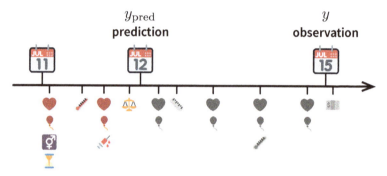

Figure 5.15   The observations in gray should never influence X.

Any values measured or observed after the moment y_{pred} is evaluated shouldn't be included in X, even during the training phase. In our example, the BMI should not be included in the features since it depends on ✎, which is typically measured *after* the prediction is made. The vital signs can be included in X if they only aggregate the values measured on the first day.

As long as you can ensure no data is leaking, extract as many features as you can. This improves the chances that your model will find good patterns to make reliable predictions. Let's now see how to choose a model and evaluate how accurate those predictions are.

5.2   Evaluation

After building X and y, the next step is to choose a model to train. The first thing you'll notice is that models are either **regressors** or **classifiers**. Regressors predict quantities, while classifiers predict labels. To predict people's nationality, you'll use a classifier. But to predict people's age, it's better to use a regressor.

Pick one of your library's models and get started. Don't worry about which specific model to choose—you can pick any. At this point, simply ensure you're picking a regressor if your y is numerical data—or a classifier if it's categorical data.

Most models use a technique called **supervised learning**. The trick is for the model to make a series of guesses on its training examples. Each time, the model will use its internal `predict` function and then evaluate how well it predicts by comparing the output y_{pred} with the true y. Using this evaluation and some math tricks, it will try to improve itself and guess again. Once the predictions stop improving, the model will stop training. The following flowchart summarizes the process:

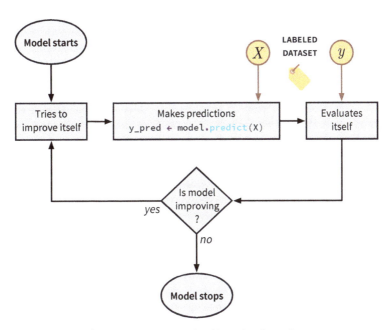

Figure 5.16 Supervised learning in action.

Now we have a trained model that we can use to predict the future. Sweet. But how well can the model predict? How can it be evaluated? There are several different evaluation metrics, which either work for regressors or for classifiers. Let's start with the former.

Evaluating Regressors

Since regressors predict quantities, a natural way to evaluate how close a given prediction y_{pred} is from the true y is to calculate the **error** between the two:

$$\text{error} = y_{pred} - y.$$

This gives one error value per row of X and y. Typically, we summarize all those errors using a type of average. Here are some common ways to do it:

MEAN ABSOLUTE ERROR (MAE) The mean is the most commonly used average. However, when calculating a mean, positive and negative errors cancel each other out and give us a false sense of precision. In order to avoid this, the **MAE** is the mean of all *absolute* errors, i.e. the mean of all errors *ignoring their negative signs*. For instance, let's suppose we're training a model to predict apartment prices in thousands of dollars, based on the labeled examples from fig. 5.2:

y_{pred}	y		Error	Abs. Error
Pred. Price	True Price			
650	840		-190	190
662	540		122	122
835	745		90	90
179	185		-6	6

$$\text{MAE} = \frac{190 + 122 + 90 + 6}{4} = 102.$$

Figure 5.17 Calculating the MAE of four predictions.

Following this method, the average error is of $102,000. If we had calculated the mean of *errors* instead of *absolute errors*, we would have obtained a misleading average of $4,000! Always ensure you sum positive values when calculating the MAE.

ROOT MEAN SQUARE ERROR (RMSE) In some cases, a single wildly inaccurate prediction may result in catastrophe. If we're sensitive to extreme errors, we can make our evaluation penalize them more by calculating the mean of the *squared* errors:

y_{pred}	y
Pred. Price	**True Price**
650	840
662	540
835	745
179	185

Error	**(Error)²**
-190	36,100
122	14,884
90	8,100
-6	36

$$\text{RMSE} = \sqrt{\frac{36100 + 14884 + 8100 + 36}{4}} \approx 122.$$

Figure 5.18 Calculating the RMSE of four predictions.

This time, the predictions yield an average error of about $121,600. Here, there is no problem with negative numbers, since the *square* of a negative number is always positive. Furthermore, the **RMSE** is the *square root* of the mean, which brings the value back to the original scale of the errors.

Let's see how the choice between MAE and RMSE affects training. Imagine that the model tried to improve itself, and now yields the following predictions:

y_{pred}	y
Pred. Price	**True Price**
748	840
650	540
887	745
281	185

Error	**Abs. Error**	**(Error)²**
-92	92	8,464
110	110	12,100
142	142	20,164
96	96	9,216

$$\text{MAE} = 110, \qquad \text{RMSE} \approx 112.$$

Figure 5.19 Evaluating new predictions using MAE and RMSE.

The MAE increased from $102,000 to $110,000, whereas the RMSE decreased from about $122,000 to about $112,000. This shows that the question "Is the model improving?" from one training iteration to the next (fig. 5.16) can be answered differently depending on which evaluation method is used.

Be careful not to compare model errors when they are predicting outputs of different scales. For example, if the same model were trained to predict the *monthly rent* of the same apartments, the MAE and RMSE would likely be around $500. These smaller scores would *not* indicate that the model got any better: they would simply translate the fact that the entire y column of labels was about 200 times smaller.

The MAE and RMSE can give some insight into a model's ability to predict the future. The better the model generalizes to new data, the closer these scores will be from the errors of future predictions.

WHAT ABOUT CLASSIFIERS? If your model is a classifier, it will output labels as it predicts, not numbers—meaning the scoring techniques we've seen cannot be used on it. Scoring a classifier can be *much* more complicated than scoring a regressor. To avoid distracting you from the main topic of how a prediction system is built, we placed our comprehensive explanation of how to score classifiers into Appendix IV. Make sure to check it out later!

5.3 Validation

Sometimes, a model is trained in a way that makes it too attached to the specific events it learned from. When that happens, the model approximates y values for records in the labeled dataset far better than for records it has never seen. This is called **overfitting**.

When we evaluate an overfitted model for the events it learned from, the resulting score is misleading. Since this is always a risk, we **validate** the model: we evaluate its predictions for events *not* used in training. This is the only way to ensure the model's score isn't deceptively good because of overfitting. The score then better reflects the model's *true performance*: the one we can expect from it when making actual predictions out in the real world.

In order to be able to validate a model, we must set aside some labeled examples *before* we start training. To that end, we split the rows of X and y into a ♠ **training set** and a ✅ **validation set**.

The model is trained using data from the training set, and scored by how it predicts the events in the validation set.

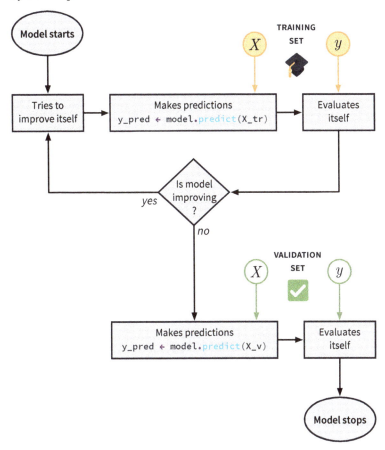

Figure 5.20 The validation set is kept aside for a final, independent evaluation of the model.

Note that rows of the labeled dataset must be split *at random*. Splitting the dataset without shuffling its rows often adds selection bias to the process.

No strict rule dictates how large each set should be. Typically, 10% to 20% of the data is reserved for validation. The bigger the training set, the better the model can learn to perform; the bigger the validation set, the more confident we are that the final score reflects the model's true performance. Still, unless the validation set is extremely large with hundreds of thousands of records, data scientists hardly ever rely solely on the single score obtained through this simple dataset split.

Unfortunately, the records we choose to include in the training or validation sets influence our final score. Often, different selections of the labeled dataset aren't equally as difficult for the model to learn from. If you evaluate the model only once, there's a risk you shuffled the rows into an atypical training or testing set—resulting in a score that doesn't reflect the model's true performance.

Cross-validation mitigates this risk by repeating the entire process several times. Each time, the labeled dataset is split into different training and validation sets. This yields many scores, which collectively describe the model's performance. Let's learn the three most common ways to perform cross-validation.

K-Folds

Instead of splitting the shuffled dataset in two—as we had done when we created a pair of training and validation sets—let's split it into ten different groups, or **folds**, of (almost) equal size:

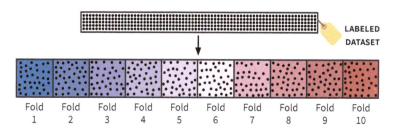

Figure 5.21 Shuffling 365 records into folds of 36 or 37 each.

Using these folds, we can construct a training set by joining the records in the first nine folds, while reserving the last for validation:

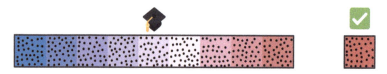

Figure 5.22 Folds 1-9 are the training set, fold 10 is the validation set.

By reserving a different fold for validation, we can construct ten different training and validation sets. This lets us evaluate our model ten different times, yielding ten different scores:

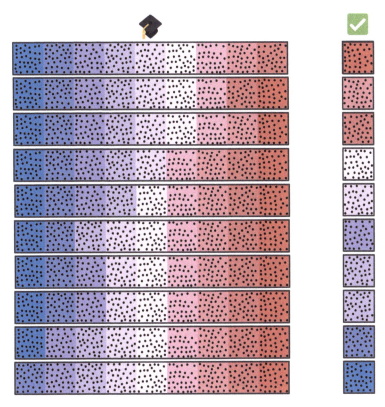

Figure 5.23   Ten different training and validation sets.

This technique is called **k-fold**, as any number of folds could have been used. With more folds, you evaluate your model more times, and the number of records in the training sets increases. However, more folds also require more computations. Also, the training sets become more similar to each other, which negates some of the advantages of evaluating the model multiple times. It's generally best to stick to the default configuration most scientists use: either five or ten folds.

Monte Carlo

With k-folds, each record gets to be in the validation set just once. This means that each record is used for model validation a single time. This can be a problem: if the model had been trained with a different selection of training data, it would likely predict some events differently. This is never explored using k-folds.

In contrast, the **Monte Carlo method** allows a single record to be in many validation sets for a more thorough validation of the model. Instead of using a fixed set of folds, it entirely re-shuffles the labeled dataset before each split. This way, it selects many random training and validation sets, then trains and scores the model for each random selection.

Monte Carlo is used when there is an abundance of computing power, and the model can be trained and scored repeatedly at little cost. If we wished to train with 90% of our 365 records and validate with the remaining 10%, Monte Carlo could evaluate the model a virtually unlimited number of times[3] with different random training and validation sets. After a few million evaluations, we can be more certain that the different scores collectively reflect the model's true performance.

Leave-One-Out

Sometimes, we have to work with a very small labeled dataset of only a few dozen records. In such cases, it makes sense to keep the training set as large as possible. To this end, we train the model on all records *but one*, and evaluate on this remaining record.

This strategy is called **leave-one-out**. It can be seen as a special case of the k-fold: there are as many folds as the total record count, so each fold contains only one record.

But there's a catch: all training instances are extremely similar to each other. Even though the model will be evaluated many times, the different evaluations are going to be very similar, nullifying some of the advantages of performing multiple evaluations.

---

[3]In theory, there are trillions of trillions *of trillions* **of trillions** of different possible validation sets that use 10% of our 365 records. Our first book, *Computer Science Distilled*, explains how to count such combinations.

Only use leave-one-out as a last resort when you cannot increase the size of your tiny dataset.

Interpretation

Cross-validation leaves you with many scores that collectively describe your model's performance. We typically summarize these values to better interpret them, for example with their five-number summary. The interpretation can depend on what you need your model to do.

If, for example, you don't mind bad performance as long as the model *sometimes* performs extremely well, focus on the upper quartile and maximum score. If, on the other hand, you cannot afford rare cases of poor model performance, take the pessimistic approach and focus on the lower quartile and minimum.

In general, the mean is taken as the most relevant summary of how the model is doing. But the mean is only a rough representation of the model's performance. It's good practice to consider it along with the standard deviation: the degree to which the model's performance typically differs from the mean.

Besides providing a measure for expected model performance, cross-validation scores also allow us to compare different models. There are many types of models with different internal mechanisms. To compare two models and decide which is best, don't look at the means. Perform a hypothesis test on the cross-validated scores from both models to check whether there's statistical significance in stating that one model has a higher mean score than the other.

Oftentimes, a computationally heavy model will have a slightly higher mean score than a simpler model. Yet, a hypothesis test will tell us that the difference isn't statistically significant. In these cases, choose the simpler model.

5.4 Fine-Tuning

We learned to prepare data, train a generic machine learning model, and measure its performance. If you stop there and don't make adjustments to your system, you will only achieve a fraction of the predictive power within your reach.

A prediction system can be tweaked in many different ways. For example, adjusting your features can dramatically improve prediction performance. Selecting the most appropriate type of model and adjusting its specific parameters for your task also helps.

Data scientists start by training and cross-validating a simple prediction model. They then make small incremental changes to their system, carrying out a new cross-validation every time. Scores before and after each change are compared, and changes that bring statistically significant improvements are kept. This process continues until no improvements to the system can be found.

Figure 5.24 "Machine Learning", courtesy of http://xkcd.com.

Let's start with the adjustments that can be made to the features. Features are most effective when they provide clear hints to the model. Your columns of X must be a collection of clues that relate to what you're predicting as directly as possible. Sometimes, transforming the values in X can help achieve this.

The process of transforming features to make them work better with a model is called **feature engineering**. Out of all adjustments that can be made to a prediction system, this one often holds the biggest potential for improvement. Let's see some of the most common feature engineering techniques.

Imputation

In Section 5.1, we said X can't contain NULL cells, and we discussed strategies to handle them: dropping rows with missing data, dropping columns with missing data, filling blank cells with a column's average, or with a default value. To discover which strategies best fit your prediction task and data, try them out and evaluate their performance!

For instance, if you're filling cells with a column's median, also try the mean, and try a constant default value. For each column that has more than 1% of NULL cells, testing the effects of a few different imputation strategies is generally worth it. If no strategy is significantly better than the others, stick with the simplest: fill all blank cells with a constant default value.

Outliers

The presence of outliers in X can confuse some models. As with the imputation of missing values, there are various ways to deal with outliers. For example, if a column only has a handful of outliers, it's often best to drop their rows from X. If outliers are frequent (for example more than 1% of the rows), you can try to replace them with less extreme values. This technique is known as **clipping**.

Figure 5.25   Clipping three outliers.

Normalization

Some models are confused by features that display widely different ranges. A feature whose values range from zero to a few thousands might receive a biased weight if the other columns range from zero to a few dozens. To prevent this issue, columns can be rescaled such that they all display a similar range. This is called **normalization** The simplest normalization technique is called **MinMax**. The minimum value in the column becomes zero, the maximum becomes one. All other values are placed in between:

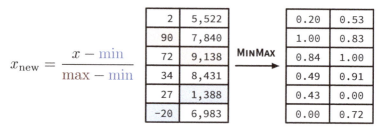

Figure 5.26 MinMax squeezes all values to the 0–1 range.

You can also normalize values according to their individual distance to the mean and the column's standard deviation: a value equal to the mean becomes zero; a value equal to the standard deviation becomes one. This normalization method is called the **z-score**:{index{z-score}

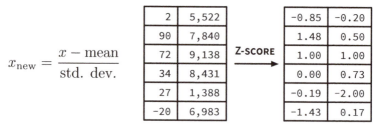

Figure 5.27 With z-score normalization, ranges aren't fixed.

When using MinMax, all columns have the *exact* same range. Moreover, the presence of outliers will force non-outliers to be squeezed closer to each other into smaller regions within the 0–1 range. Using z-scores, outliers have less influence since they don't cause this squeezing, and the ranges of non-outliers are more similar between columns. To find out which normalization method to use, try both and compare cross-validation results.

Log Transformation

In Section 4.4, we plotted the decreasing costs of computer storage over the past decades and discovered that data spanning several orders of magnitude can need special handling. The same is true for feeding this type of data to predictive models. Features with huge variance often weaken predictive performance.

If your X table has such columns, try transforming their values using a logarithmic function (log). If there are values between zero and one in the column, add one before calculating the logarithm in order to avoid large negative outputs.

If the column also includes negative numbers, the transformation gets trickier, as logarithms aren't defined for such numbers. One way to get around this is to remove the minus sign, add one, apply the logarithm, and reapply the minus sign:

$$x_{\log} = \begin{cases} \log(x+1) & \text{if } x \geq 0, \\ -1 \times \log((-1 \times x) + 1) & \text{otherwise.} \end{cases}$$

In addition, you may normalize a column right after performing a logarithmic transformation to it. Here's an example:

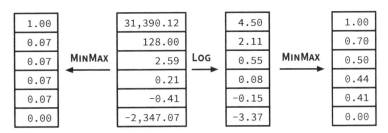

Figure 5.28 MinMax with and without prior log transformation.

Directly normalizing data with extreme variance leads to a lot of values being very close to each other. By performing a logarithmic transformation before the normalization, numbers are better spread across the range, and differences between values are easier for the model to perceive.

Binning

Making a feature carry *less* information sometimes helps the model. Suppose your hospital is trying to predict the duration of stay of incoming patients, and that you have a column for their age. As you investigate, you notice that small age differences have little effect on the duration of hospitalizations, yet there is a significant difference between children and adults. In this case, try to help the model differentiate these groups. For example, you can transform age into a categorical feature with the labels "child", "teen" and "adult".

This technique is called **binning**. It consists of organizing the original data into "bins" which are more relevant than the original values. It can also be helpful when you have categorical features where some labels rarely appear—study them and bin the related ones together.

For instance, a categorical feature indicating a patient's disease may have thousands of labels. Binning them in groups of related diseases can help the model make sense of the data. If you don't have time to create elaborate bins, try simply replacing all low-frequency labels with a single "others" label. That alone can potentially help your model a lot.

Clustering

In hospitals, incoming patients are often assigned to a group according to their symptoms or illness. This helps doctors and nurses: they can check which group a patient belongs to and obtain instant, valuable information about the patient.

If you are a restaurant's manager, it can also be useful to divide customers into groups. There are the junkie diners, the healthy food lovers, the penny-pinchers, etc. Knowing these groups allows you to target different promotions to the customers who are most likely to respond. Also, the restaurant may adapt its offerings to its most profitable customers.

Be careful: you must group elements judiciously for it to help your model. Most datasets will contain sets of rows with similar characteristics. If you manage to group records according to these similarities, add a column to X indicating which group each record is a part of. This new categorical feature will often enhance the performance of a predictive model.

The process of finding similar characteristics and assigning each record to a group is called **clustering**. There are algorithms that can automate clustering. The most widely used clustering algorithm is called **k-means**. Install a library that has this algorithm, and run it on your dataset. In addition to X, the algorithm requires you to input k, the number of different groups it should create. To get started, run it multiple times, setting k from 2 to 10. Each time, you should obtain a different extra column for X. Cross-validate the model for each grouping, and keep the one that helps your model the most.

If you are using an automatically generated grouping of rows as a new feature, there's an interesting data exploration exercise you can do. Look into the records assigned to each group, and try to come up with a name that best represents it. This game will sometimes lead you to interesting discoveries!

Feature Extraction

As we collect features, X may end up having columns which highly correlate to each other. When this happens, redundant information is being passed to the model, which in most cases is not very useful. Most models work best when each column of X carries distinct information. Fortunately, there are special math tricks that allow you to compress the information contained in a group of columns into fewer, more representative features. This process is called **feature extraction**.

A well-known feature extraction trick is the Principal Component Analysis, or **PCA**.[4] It requires columns in X to be normalized via z-score first. PCA transforms some columns into less correlated columns that preserve the original information. Let's see an example where columns store the average, minimum and maximum daily temperatures in a city:

---

[4]For an interactive explanation of PCA, see http://code.energy/pca.

	Z-SCORE			PCA	

T_{avg}	T_{max}	T_{min}	T_{avg}	T_{max}	T_{min}	c_1	c_2	c_3
6.9	7.8	5.0	1.06	0.61	-1.70	-1.93	-0.80	-0.03
6.6	10.6	-0.5	0.97	-1.00	0.03	-1.37	0.94	-0.01
-1.0	1.7	-3.8	-1.16	0.61	-0.98	1.81	-0.01	0.09
4.3	7.8	1.7	0.33	0.74	0.69	-0.94	-0.12	0.27
6.3	8.3	1.1	0.89	-0.87	0.51	-1.25	0.18	-0.15
1.2	2.2	-2.1	-0.54	2.2	-0.46	1.08	-0.24	-0.18
-2.4	0.0	-5.5	-1.55	-1.45	-1.49	2.59	0.06	0.01

Correlation

T_{avg}/T_{max}	0.96	T_{avg}/T_{max}	0.96	c_1/c_2	0.00
T_{avg}/T_{min}	0.88	T_{avg}/T_{min}	0.88	c_1/c_3	0.00
T_{max}/T_{min}	0.77	T_{max}/T_{min}	0.77	c_2/c_3	0.00

Standard Deviation

T_{avg}	3.85	T_{avg}	1.08	c_1	1.79
T_{max}	4.08	T_{max}	1.08	c_2	0.52
T_{min}	3.56	T_{min}	1.08	c_3	0.15

Figure 5.29 Features transformed via z-scores and PCA. At each step, the correlation coefficient between columns is shown, as well as each column's standard deviation.

PCA returns a new X where columns display little correlation with each other. Furthermore, PCA tends to compact more information in the columns to the left and orders them by decreasing levels of variance. We can then try to discard the columns to the right, which display little variance, and see if the model performs better. It often does!

Another feature extraction trick is the **Non-negative Matrix Factorization**, or **NMF**. As its name suggests, it only works if X contains no negative values. It allows us to compress the information of X into a number of columns of our choosing. Let's use NMF to transform the data from our previous example into two columns:

MinMax			NMF(2)				

T_{avg}	T_{max}	T_{min}	T_{avg}	T_{max}	T_{min}	c_1	c_2
6.9	7.8	5.0	1.00	0.74	1.00	0.67	0.67
6.6	10.6	-0.5	0.97	1.00	0.48	0.91	0.00
-1.0	1.7	-3.8	0.15	0.16	0.16	0.13	0.09
4.3	7.8	1.7	0.72	0.74	0.69	0.62	0.34
6.3	8.3	1.1	0.93	0.78	0.63	0.74	0.27
1.2	2.2	-2.1	0.39	0.21	0.32	0.22	0.24
-2.4	0.0	-5.5	0.00	0.00	0.00	0.00	0.00

Correlation

T_{avg}/T_{max}	0.96		T_{avg}/T_{max}	0.96	c_1/c_2	0.34
T_{avg}/T_{min}	0.88		T_{avg}/T_{min}	0.88		
T_{max}/T_{min}	0.77		T_{max}/T_{min}	0.77		

Standard Deviation

T_{avg}	3.85		T_{avg}	0.41	c_1	0.35
T_{max}	4.08		T_{max}	0.48	c_2	0.24
T_{min}	3.56		T_{min}	0.34		

Figure 5.30 Features transformed via MinMax and NMF. At each step, the correlation coefficient between columns is shown, as well as each column's standard deviation.

Unlike PCA, NMF generated unordered columns that are all equally relevant. While PCA outputs a series of columns of diminishing relevance, NMF attempts to split information into columns representing distinct behaviors. As usual, it's helpful to experiment with different numbers of output columns. Test your model with NMF tables of different sizes, and pick the number that works best.

Before PCA or NMF, columns of X typically represent a specific measurement or attribute. After either transformation, columns no longer have a direct link to an attribute from the real world, even though they collectively retain the original information. This may help a machine, but it makes the data less transparent to humans. For this reason, feature extraction is usually the last step of the feature engineering process.

Feature Selection

Some features might hinder a model's performance rather than help it. This often happens with redundant features, features containing bad quality data, or features that aren't really related to y. Removing unhelpful columns from X is called **feature selection**.

Model performance will vary when we use different subsets of features and want to select the subset that maximizes performance. The only way to guarantee this is to evaluate all possible selections of columns, keeping track of the best selection found. That's called an **exhaustive search**, and it's only doable if X has few columns. With many features, the number of subsets to evaluate explodes.[5]

In these cases, we select features via *heuristic methods*: methods that lead to a solution without guaranteeing it is the best or optimal one. The simplest such method is called **backward elimination**. We keep checking if removing one of the features improves performance. If it does, the feature is dropped. Once we've tried removing all features without success, we stop and keep the features that remained:

```
keep_changing ← True
while(keep_changing)
    keep_changing ← False
    for each column in X
        X_new ← X.remove(column)
        if is_better(X_new, X)
            X ← X_new
            keep_changing ← True
            break
```

The reverse process is called **forward selection**: start with an empty feature set and keep adding new features one-by-one, as long as they improve performance. When there's a tie between selecting a larger or a smaller group of features, opt for the smaller option.[6]

There are many more feature selection strategies. They will generally make a model simpler and faster, in addition to improving its performance.

---

[5]The number of subsets from a set with n elements is 2^n.

[6]Backward elimination and forward selection are forms of *greedy* heuristic methods we described in our first book, *Computer Science Distilled*.

Data Leakage, Again

We've seen that our labeled dataset has to be split into training and validation sets in order to evaluate a model. Since the validation set is used to gauge the model's true performance outside of its training realm, it should never affect the training of the model.

This also applies to feature engineering: all transformations will affect the training of the model, and therefore must be calibrated *only* using the training set. Failing to do so amounts to *data leakage*, as described in Section 5.1. Let's go through some examples to make sure you get the idea.

Suppose you're performing mean imputation to one of your columns. The mean values are calculated from the rows of the training set only. The blank cells of the training and validation sets will both be filled with the mean *of the training set*. This way, no information from the validation set leaks into the training set.

Similarly, you must always decide which values are considered outliers based on the training set only. After this decision is made, apply the exact same numerical operations to both training and validation sets.

When normalizing via MinMax, use the training set's minimum and maximum values as your reference for transforming both the training and the validation sets. If you're normalizing via z-scores, consider the training set's mean and standard deviation. When developing binning strategies, consider the occurrence of labels in the training set only to decide how your data should be categorized.

The same rules apply for feature extraction: the PCA or NMF algorithm should be calibrated using the training set. The exact same mathematical operations will then be performed on both training and validation sets.

We've seen that the training set changes for each independent evaluation during cross-validation. This means your feature engineering transformations should be re-calibrated and applied to each new pair of training and validation sets. Watch out: don't calibrate and apply feature engineering transformations only once and before cross-validation, but rather many times *during* cross-validation. It's a common mistake that often leads to inaccurate predictions down the line.

Model Selection

Open source machine learning libraries are available for most modern programming languages. These libraries usually come preloaded with dozens of different models you can readily put to use.

Each different model employs different mathematical tricks to train and predict. As you become a seasoned machine learning practitioner, you'll eventually learn how models work and behave in different situations. This experience will help you use different models more effectively.

If you're getting started with machine learning, it's OK to try all available models in your machine learning library, even if you have no clue how they work under the hood. As you try them, you'll empirically discover which ones are best for the predictive tasks you're working on.

There's just one thing you must research about every model you use: its configuration settings known as **hyperparameters**. They should be adjusted to your prediction task. Sticking to default settings often results in bad performance and prevents you from fairly evaluating a model's potential.

In order to properly adjust your hyperparameters, start by checking the model's documentation. Once you know what your options are, start experimenting. For example, you could try doubling or halving the default values of each hyper-parameter and see how it affects performance. Keep tinkering with the hyperparameters until you're confident you've found the right setting for each.[7] After you've adjusted the hyperparameters of each model you intend to evaluate, you can compare their performance and finally select the one that works best.

Final Steps

After you adjust your features and model, it's time to prepare the system for real world deployment. Since you've already decided

---

[7]When you gain some experience, you'll discover methods that automatically search through many hyperparameter settings for a given model and select the best one automatically.

all of your adjustments, you don't need a validation set anymore. Take all of your imputation, outlier handling, normalization, and binning rules, as well as your feature extraction transformations, and calibrate them using your *entire* labeled dataset.

The next step is to take your chosen model with its ideal hyper-parameters and train it using your *entire* labeled dataset. Combined, your feature transformation rules and your trained model are your final prediction system, ready to be put to use.

Once a new, never-before-seen event happens, feed its features to the system. If you did everything right, it will output a glimpse of the event's unknown future. That glimpse will be as accurate as you have evaluated the model's performance to be via cross-validation... Or will it?

Unfortunately, since you've been using the entire dataset over and over to adjust your system, there's still a possibility that some overfitting has crept in during the fine-tuning phase. This means that your system is adjusted to your dataset better than it would be to any other events. In other words, it will perform better on records of your labeled dataset than on never-before-seen events.

TEST SET   The only way to ensure a completely unbiased evaluation of a predictive system is to evaluate it with data it has never been in contact with. To this end, we could have separated a small part of our labeled dataset into a **test set** before we had even started with cross-validation. The test set is *never* used for training, validation, or final preparation of the model. It is only used for a single, ultimate evaluation of the model that will go live. If the labeled data is unbiased, the model's performance on the test set should be a true sample of its performance in the real world.

Conclusion

Building a machine learning system is an intricate process. There are many details you must get right to obtain usable predictive results. So take advantage of existing libraries: they will help you perform feature engineering, cross-validation, and model evaluation. Many of them can do nearly everything we saw in this chapter.

When using such libraries, data transformations and cross-validation steps only take a few lines of code. It's common for programmers to use code notebooks to share this type of code. Code notebooks mix text, code, and plots in the same file, and can easily be viewed, re-executed and experimented with.

The reproducibility principle that was discussed at length in the previous chapter also applies to machine learning. Make sure all transformations of your data are reproducible and structured in a pipeline that's easy to modify. The same goes for processes to fine-tune your model and its hyperparameters.

Keep in mind that this was an introduction to the practice of machine learning. There are many tricks we didn't mention. For instance, there are techniques for combining the prediction results of different models into a so-called *ensemble*, which often outperforms any individual model.

Machine learning is developing at a fast pace. New techniques for feature engineering and model selection are published every year, and big tech companies are now offering cloud computing services with automated platforms for predictive model creation. By practicing the concepts presented in this chapter, you'll be able to make the best use of these resources... and make sense of the artificial intelligence revolution as it unfolds.

Figure 5.31   Machine learning doesn't solve everything.

It can be scary to think that machines are influencing our decisions—or that they are outright making them for us. Whenever a prediction might influence someone's life, think of the possible consequences. Machine learning is neither good nor evil: it's your job to use it ethically and responsibly.

Reference

- Machine Learning for Absolute Beginners, by Theobald
  - Get it at https://code.energy/theobald
- The Data Science Design Manual, by Skiena
  - Get it at https://code.energy/skiena
- Deep Learning, by Goodfellow
  - Get it at https://code.energy/goodfellow
- The Elements of Statistical Learning, by Tibshirani
  - Get it at https://code.energy/tibshirani
- Prof. Raschka's paper on Model Evaluation and Selection
  - Get it at https://code.energy/raschka

CONCLUSION

> We have actually succeeded in making our discipline
> a science, and in a remarkably simple way: merely
> by deciding to call it 'computer science'.
>
> —DONALD KNUTH

This book presented ways in which computer science unleashed powers that enabled programmers to build the digital world we live in. By using these concepts yourself to play with networks and data science, you will contribute to an even more resourceful society.

We tried to limit the depth of our exploration to an introductory level. The goal was to show you the essentials that everyone who works with code should know. We hope to have sparked your curiosity to keep exploring with the books referenced at the end of each chapter. You will also find after this conclusion a bonus chapter about regular expressions: a technique for searching patterns which will help you with the processing steps of any data analysis or machine learning task.

We wanted to include more topics in this book, but it grew too large. For instance, when presenting machine learning, we skipped the algorithms that enable computers to gather knowledge without human supervision. And we haven't talked about cloud computing, which enables new worlds to be created much faster. Stay tuned if you're interested in these topics—we might cover them in an upcoming book! If you bought this book from Code Energy, you will receive announcement emails from us. Otherwise, you can sign up to receive our updates at http://code.energy/list.

Hopefully, this book improved your theoretical understanding of computational systems. Now, it's time to get out there and play! Start a new coding project and practice what you learned. As a wise coder once said:

> *"If you find that you're spending almost all your time on theory, start turning some attention to practical things; it*

will improve your theories. If you find that you're spending almost all your time on practice, start turning some attention to theoretical things; it will improve your practice."

Lastly, don't hesitate to send us your feedback on the book: email us at hi@code.energy. The feedback we received from our first book, *Computer Science Distilled*, motivated us to write this one and brought our attention to details in our writing style that could be improved. Thank you!

BONUS

Patterns

> Regular expressions allow you to master your data. Control it. Put it to work for you. To master regular expressions is to master your data.
>
> —JEFFREY FRIEDL

CODERS OFTEN WORK with data that matches a given pattern. Let's consider a document containing dates written as "Feb 27th 2013", "27/2/13" and "2013-02-27". How do we find all the dates in such a file? Writing programs to detect patterns is time-consuming and quite tedious.

Figure 7.1   Don't ask your boss on a date!

Thankfully, we can define patterns of text such as date formats using **regular expressions**. These expressions can then be interpreted by existing software so we don't have to write the pattern-matching code ourselves. In this chapter, we'll learn to:

- •• **Match** basic patterns,
- Precisely **quantify** repeating patterns,
- ⚓ **Anchor** patterns to locations,
- Capture **groups** of items within a pattern.

223

Regular expressions are also referred to as **regex** or **regexp**. They are tremendous time-savers loved by most programmers. They are easy to integrate in your code thanks to the many readily available libraries and tools. In fact, they are already built in most programming languages, source code editors, command line tools, etc.

Figure 7.2 *"I used to be a big stuttering piece of code. Now I'm sharp and clear, and I easily find dates!"*

Matching

A regular expression is like a search term on steroids. Consider the following line:

```
District 1, Paris
```

That's a simple regular expression, and it works as a typical search. A **regular expression engine** is a program that will interpret this expression, run it against some text, and report a match if the string "District 1, Paris" can be found. There are slight variations in syntax, features, and behaviors across engines. Nerds call them **flavors**.

Most flavors are case-sensitive by default, so "district 1, paris" would not have been matched. Fortunately, they also allow you to configure the way they crunch data through **flags**. For example, the **case insensitive** flag (typically denoted i) would allow us to find "district 1, paris" from our capitalized expression.[1]

We *strongly* encourage you to try all the regular expressions in this chapter. Open http://code.energy/regex and you'll see a field for your regular expression, and a text box for a test input. It will show where the expression matches the input. You can also set flags. Try it and observe how the case insensitive flag affects your matches!

The Dot

Let's suppose you want to search for any of these phrases:

- "District 1, Paris",
- "District 2, Paris",
- "District 3, Paris",
- "District 4, Paris".

Instead of carrying out four searches, we can let the tenth character of a single search match anything:

```
District ., Paris
```

In regular expressions, the **dot** (.) has a special meaning: it will match any single character. Our expression will even match phrases we're not interested in such as "District 0, Paris" and "District !, Paris". Nevertheless, the dot provides a quick way to find text that loosely matches your pattern. Consider this expression:

```
c.........y
```

It matches "calligraphy", "consistency", and "chaotically", and since the dot also matches the space character, "can be easy" and

---

[1]The way to set flags varies across flavors. Flags are sometimes appended after a forward slash, for instance District 1, Paris/i.

"code energy" are also matched. Note that boundaries between words aren't considered here, so "cisco enjoy" will be found in "Francisco enjoyed". Let's see how all this allows us to do far more than a static search:

> DOMAIN NAME 🌐 You remember an email mentioning a website that ends with `mil` and a country code. You don't remember much else: it could be `mil.br/`, `eng.mil.ru/`, `mil.be/frite`, etc. How can you find the domain?

All country code top-level domains have two characters. The dot matches any character, even an actual period. This expression will find all possible matches:

```
mil.../
```

The dot is mostly used for quick, dirty work and it typically finds much more than we're expecting. Let's now see how to be *very* specific with regular expressions.

The Set

A term written inside [●●●] brackets is called a **set**. A set works like a dot, though it will only match one of the characters contained in its brackets. Replace the dot with a set and our search for Parisian districts becomes exact:

```
District [1234], Paris
```

This will *only* match the four cases in which we're interested. Such ranges of characters are often used in sets, and so there exists a shorthand to make them compact and easy to read:

- [1-4] is equivalent to [1234],
- [h-p] is equivalent to [hijklmnop].

This improves our solution to the Domain Name problem 🌐:

```
mil.[a-z][a-z]/
```

A set can contain multiple ranges. For instance, the following regular expression matches a character that is either in the 0-9 range or in the A-F range. In other words, it matches a hex digit:[2]

```
[A-F0-9]
```

By stacking a # and six of these sets, we can match hex color codes,[3] such as #E67F31:

```
#[A-F0-9][A-F0-9][A-F0-9][A-F0-9][A-F0-9][A-F0-9]
```

Some sets are very common in regular expressions. Lazy programmers defined **shorthands** for matching a digit and for matching an alphanumeric character:

- \d is equivalent to [0-9],
- \w is equivalent to [A-Za-z0-9_].[4]

In order to match a ten digit phone number (e.g. 307-555-0177), we'd have to repeat [0-9] ten times. Repeating the shorthand is more compact:

```
\d\d\d-\d\d\d-\d\d\d\d
```

We will soon discover even better ways to repeat sets.

---

[2]In hex, a single digit is a value from 0 to 15. Since we ran out of Hindu-Arabic numerals, the letters a-f are used as numerals for values 10 to 15. For more about hexadecimal digits, see the Appendix I.

[3]The symbol # followed by three pairs of hex digits is a common way to encode colors. Each pair indicates the amount of red, green, or blue light it is made of. For instance, #FF0000 indicates maximum red light, but no green or blue lights. Googling such a string will immediately return you the corresponding color!

[4]Notably, \w includes the underscore. The underscore is allowed in source code variable names, so programmers can have variables like beer_count. Adding the underscore to \w makes it easier to match variable names in source files.

The Negated Set

We sometimes want to match *almost* any character. Rather than listing the many accepted characters in a set, we list the characters that are *not* accepted in a **negated set**. It's the opposite of a set in that it matches any character that is *not* listed within its brackets. It looks like a normal set, but with a caret after the first bracket: [^•••].

> TRADING 💱 You have a list of currencies, each written as a three-letter code, such as JPY (¥), USD ($), and GPB (£). Some of these are special currencies, such as XBT (Bitcoin) and XAU (Gold). The special ones always start with X. List all non-special currency codes.

Using sets, we'd have to list every letter:

`[A-WY-Z][A-Z][A-Z]`

Matching anything that isn't an X to the first character is simpler:

`[^X][A-Z][A-Z]`

Note that this will also match "0AA", ".AA", or " AA", as the negated list matches *any character* that's not in its brackets. Whether or not `[^X][A-Z][A-Z]` will only match actual currency codes depends on our input. Negated sets are also useful for catching things we didn't expect:

> PROOFREADING 🔎 While reviewing this book, we had to check that every punctuation mark is followed by a space. How did we search for this kind of goof?

If there is anything other than a space after a punctuation character, we can match it and review it:

`[.,:;?!][^ ]`

Did you notice that we're using a period character inside the set, and that it matches an actual period? That's because characters inside the set lose their special powers. Let's now learn to do this outside of sets.

Special Characters

To make a special character[5] lose its regex functionality, we use \, the **escape character.**\index{escape character@escape character } For instance, \. matches an actual period character—it's the same as [.]. The Domain Name problem ⊕ now has an even more precise solution:

```
mil\.[a-z][a-z]/
```

Other characters can also be expressed with an escape sequence. This comes in handy when matching non-printable characters:

- \t matches a tab,
- \n matches a new line,
- \r matches a carriage return (useful in Windows),
- \f matches a page break,
- \s is equivalent to [\t\r\n\f].

The shorthand \s is called **whitespace.** Note that it includes the regular space character! This allows us to improve the solution to the Proofreading problem 🔍 so it doesn't waste our time returning punctuation followed by new lines and page breaks:

```
[.,:;?!][^\s]
```

With dots, sets, negated sets, special characters and shorthands, we can now flexibly match individual characters. But what if we don't know exactly how many characters we're looking for?

---

[5]These guys: . ? * + ^ $ | [ ] { } ( ) \.

Quantifiers

In our previous expression matching ten digit phone numbers, the repeating \d are bulky and hard to read. To simplify, we can use **quantifiers** that change the number of characters a \d will match.

Curly Braces

We can specify exactly how many times a character or set of characters must match using **curly braces**. For instance, the regular expression that matched ten-digit phone numbers can be rewritten:

```
\d{3}-\d{3}-\d{4}
```

This expression is equivalent to \d\d\d-\d\d\d-\d\d\d\d, only cleaner. It reads "match three digits, then a dash, then three digits, then a dash, then four digits". A quantifier can also be used to improve the expression that finds hexadecimal color codes:

```
#[A-F0-9]{6}
```

Components of the expression match exactly once by default, so {1} has no effect: B{1}e{2}r{1} is the same as Beer. Moreover, besides these *fixed* match requirements, we can also specify a *range*. It's possible to state a minimum or a maximum number of matches:

- exactly n times: {n},
- at least n times, and at most m times: {n,m},
- at least n times, with no upper limit: {n,}.

Note that n can be zero, effectively making the beer optional.

> MESSY NUMBERS 🇧🇷 Brazilian phone numbers have variable lengths. The area code has two digits, and the local number can have eight or nine digits. Also, the dash before the last four digits is sometimes omitted. How can we find these numbers in a document?

We can use one range quantifier to specify the number of acceptable digits and another to make the second dash optional:

`\d{2}-\d{4,5}-{0,1}\d{4}`

This expression can seem intimidating, so let's decode it bit by bit:

- `\d{2}` matches two digits,
- `-` matches a single dash,
- `\d{4,5}` matches four or five digits,
- `-{0,1}` matches no dashes or a single dash,
- `\d{4}` matches four digits.

The Optional

The quantifier we used to make the dash optional in our last expression is so common that there exists a shorthand. We can replace `{0,1}` with `?`. The phone expression now reads:

`\d{2}-\d{4,5}-?\d{4}`

The `?` is called the **optional**. Whether the character that immediately precedes the `?` is actually there doesn't matter, the match happens regardless. The optional is useful when looking for web URLs that may or may not use encryption:[6]

`https?://code\.energy`

This finds both http://code.energy and https://code.energy.

The Plus

The **plus** (+) is another useful shorthand. It's the same as `{1,}`, indicating something must appear at least once, with no upper limit. For instance:

---

[6]Recall from Chapter 3 that `https` is used in a URL instead of `http` to indicate it should be accessed using SSL encryption.

```
du+de
```

This matches "dude", "duude", "duuude", and so forth. If we want to catch links to any .com domain:[7]

```
https?://[a-z0-9-]+\.com
```

The Star

The most powerful quantifier is the **star** (*). It's equivalent to {0,} and combines the effect of the optional and the plus. It denotes an optional term that can occur unlimited times. For example:

```
yea*h
```

This matches "yeh", "yeah", "yeaah", "yeaaah", and so on. A dot and a star (.*) will match anything: it will accept any character, any number of times. If you think your input contains the word "restaurant", some random text, and then the word "London", you can try to find:

```
restaurant.*London
```

The .* will take care of any text between the two words. You can also use this trick to match any quote:

```
".*"
```

Greediness

The last regular expression (".*") has a problem. Test it with the following input:

Avaritia porro "hominem" ad quod "vis maleficium" impellit.

---

[7]This expression would also match some invalid domains, because the dash isn't allowed at the start or end of the name. To handle that, we need an advanced regex feature called lookarounds. Learn more at http://code.energy/lookaround.

Quantifiers are **greedy**: they try to consume as many characters as possible.[8] The dot and the star will run from the first quotation mark of our input to the last, returning:

"hominem" ad quod "vis maleficium"

To match only "hominem" , replace the dot with a negated set:

`"[^"]*"`

By default, regular expression engines will return their first match. To get multiple matches, there's the **global flag**, usually denoted **g**. It would make our last search match both "hominem" and "vis maleficium". Note that a character cannot be part of two matches, therefore this would *not* return " ad quod ".

Anchors

So far, our regular expressions could match characters and phrases anywhere in the input. **Anchors** control exactly *where* matches are allowed. Anchors don't consume characters, rather they restrict the possible positions for matches.

The Caret

When used outside brackets, the **caret** (^) restricts matches to the start of a line. Consider the following expression:

`^Once upon a time`

It will only match the start of a line that introduces a fairy tale. Many coders use a sequence of dashes (----) to create horizontal separators in plain text files. We can find them with this expression:

`^-+`

It matches a sequence of dashes, but only if it starts a line.

---

[8]Many flavors also offer **lazy** quantifiers as an alternative. Lazy quantifiers will consume as few characters as possible.

The Dollar

The **dollar** anchors the match to the end of a line. For example, take the following expression:

```
happily ever after\.$
```

It will only match a line that finishes with a happy ending. You can use both anchors in the same expression. This one searches for a fairy tale:[9]

```
^Once upon a time.*happily ever after\.$
```

We can update our expression that finds separators made of dashes to match lines that *only* contain dashes:

```
^-+$
```

Can you guess how to match an empty line? Hint: you just need two anchors in your expression.

> CLEAN CODE ✎ In most programming languages, ending a line of code with a space is frowned upon, as it serves no purpose. How can you find these "trailing spaces"?

Finding trailing spaces is simple—we match one space or more at the end of a line:

```
 +$
```

THE MULTILINE FLAG In some flavors, the caret and dollar refer to the beginning and end of the entire input: they ignore line breaks. To change this behavior, there's the **multiline** flag, typically denoted m. It will force carets and dollars to recognize new line characters.

---

[9]In most flavors, the dot will only match a new line character if the s flag is used. Use that flag to find a fairy tale spanning multiple paragraphs!

The Boundary

Some words are embedded in others. For instance, searching for fun will match characters within "<u>fun</u>eral", and searching for rude will also find "p<u>rude</u>nt". These are called **koala words**.[10] Take the following search:

art   M<u>art</u>ial <u>art</u>s imp<u>art</u> <u>art</u>ists as <u>art</u>.

What if we're just looking for the word "art"? The **boundary** anchor (\b) solves this by restricting matches to the start or end of a word:

\bart   Martial <u>art</u>s impart <u>art</u>ists as <u>art</u>.

art\b   Martial arts imp<u>art</u> artists as <u>art</u>.

\bart\b   Martial arts impart artists as <u>art</u>.

\barts?\b   Martial <u>arts</u> impart artists as <u>art</u>.

In the last expression, the plural form is an accepted koala word. If we are only interested in words that start with an **a** and end with an **s**, then we use a set and a plus or star:

\ba[a-z]+s\b   Martial <u>arts</u> impart <u>artists</u> as art.

\ba[a-z]*s\b   Martial <u>arts</u> impart <u>artists</u> <u>as</u> art.

Don't let the koalas confuse you. Anchor your expressions.

---

[10]We made that up. 🐨

Groups

As yet, we have only seen quantifiers work on a single preceding character. **Groups** allow quantifiers to work on a sequence of characters, or even on an entire expression. They are created using parenthesis: (•••). For example:

```
(meta-)*analysis
```

Here, the `meta-` part of the expression can theoretically match zero to infinite times. The expression finds "analysis", "meta-analysis", "meta-meta-analysis", and so on.

> BIG NUMBERS 🔢 You need to find big numbers in a long report. Commas separate thousands, and some numbers have fractional digits. How to retrieve all the numbers?

We could be lazy and try:

```
\b[0-9,.]+\b
```

However, this would also match other things, such as "10.12.1815". To retrieve numbers that use dots and commas correctly, we can use groups with quantifiers:

```
\b\d{1,3}(,\d{3})*(\.\d+)?\b
```

Let's parse that expression from left to right:

`\b`	The match must start at a word boundary.
`\d{1,3}`	Maximum three leftmost digits.
`(,\d{3})*`	Optionally, a comma followed by three digits.[11]
`(\.\d+)?`	Optionally, a dot followed by at least one digit.
`\b`	The match must end at a word boundary.

---

[11] Can be repeated unlimited times to match thousands, millions, billions, etc.

Capturing Groups

Groups are also called **capturing groups**: the regular expression engine keeps the text they matched as internal variables. These variables are often used to create elaborate find-and-replace schemes.

> QUIRKY QUOTES 🖊 A French translator handed you a text that includes quotes made with straight quotation marks, "like this". He asks you to replace them with French *guillemets*, for the quotes to look « like this ».

You can't directly find-and-replace the " character. It has to become either a « or a » character, depending on its position. If we add a group to our previous regular expression that finds quotation marks, the text inside the quotation mark is stored in an internal variable, called \1. We can tell the regular expression engine to replace the matched string with a new text that makes use of this variable:

Find: `"([^"]*)"`

Replace: `« \1 »`

If the regular expression has multiple groups, more capture variables are created. To reformat US telephone numbers separated with spaces using parenthesis and hyphens, you can do this:

Find: `(\d{3}) (\d{3}) (\d{4})`

Replace: `(\1) \2-\3`

Here, \1 stores the text that was matched inside the first group, \2 stores the text from the second group, and so on. Whenever you need to do a find-and-replace operation that's not static, remember to use groups!

The Alternation

When we want to match one of several expressions, we use the **alternation**, denoted |. It works similarly to a logical OR. For example, to match phone numbers only from Puerto Rico, we need one of these two area codes:

```
(787|939)-\d{3}-\d{4}
```

Notice that we confined the alternation within a group because it has lowest precedence. In other words, removing the parentheses:

```
787|939-\d{3}-\d{4}
```

is equivalent to

```
(787)|(939-\d{3}-\d{4})
```

This is wrong: the machine will read "match **787**, or a ten-digit phone number starting with **939**". Always be careful when using the alternation outside a group. Let's try another example.

> MARSUPIAL MATES 🦘 A ranger in the Australian Outback is studying kangaroo breeding behavior. Her agency monitors their population and dates its statistics in a **Mon YY** format. She knows kangaroo births peak in summer months. How can she search the data for these summer statistics?

The search must be restricted to the summer months of the Southern Hemisphere: December, January, and February:

```
(Dec|Jan|Feb) \d\d
```

If our ranger is researching one specific summer, she would have to drop the parentheses and specify the years:

```
Dec 92|Jan 93|Feb 93
```

Here, using the two groups (Dec|Jan|Feb) (92|93) is too broad. It would match months covering three summers: ~~Jan 92,~~ ~~Feb 92,~~ Dec 92, Jan 93, Feb 93, ~~Dec 93~~.

Conclusion

In this chapter, we learned how to concisely search for elaborate patterns. We've observed how regular expressions are built from a combination of characters, some representing themselves, some representing special functions. You should use these tools when:

- You must validate that an input matches an expected format (e.g. phone number, date, IP address, credit card number),
- You don't know the exact sequence of characters you're looking for, but you know how it should appear,
- You must perform complicated find-and-replace operations.

If you're working on a generic pattern, such as an IP address or a phone number, you can find ready-to-use regular expressions online. There are many regular expression libraries and cookbooks that will help you find common patterns.

When designing your own expression, start with something simple that broadly matches what you search and from there, refine your expression to be more and more specific.

Nearly all programming languages and tools support regular expressions, but be careful: there are many subtle variations across flavors. Some will interpret parentheses as literal characters, and thus require you to type \(•••\) instead of (•••) to create a group. Some older engines lack support for certain anchors, such as the word boundary. And how do we go about matching Japanese characters? The conceptual understanding you gained from this chapter will help you navigate reference material and online resources on regular expressions to find answers.

Install a regular expression extension on your browser now, so you can test it on web pages. Additionally, find how to use regular expressions in your source code editor. To write this book, we used one called Vim, that carries out *all* searches through regular expressions. If there is a way to make regular expressions the default search mode of your editor, do it—that will force you to practice them and you will save time in the long run.

Figure 7.3 "Regular Expressions", courtesy of http://xkcd.com.

Even if you're not involved in a hasty crime investigation (fig. 7.3), having quick access to specific information is essential to work efficiently. The better you are with regular expressions, the faster you can retrieve the data you need, learn them and save hours of valuable coding time.

Reference

- Mastering Regular Expressions, by Friedl
    - Get it at https://code.energy/friedl
- Regular Expressions Cookbook, by Goyvaerts and Levithan
    - Get it at https://code.energy/goyvaerts

Appendix

I Numerical Bases

Computing can be reduced to operating with numbers, because information is expressible in numbers. Letters can be mapped to numbers, so text can be written numerically. Colors are a combination of light intensities of red, blue and green, which can be given as numbers. Images can be composed by mosaics of colored squares, so they can be expressed as numbers.

Archaic number systems (e.g., roman numerals: I, II, III, …) compose numbers from sums of digits. The number system used today is also based on sums of digits, but the value of each digit in position i is multiplied by d to the power of i, where d is the number of distinct digits. We call d the **base**. We normally use $d = 10$ because we have ten fingers, but the system works for any base d:

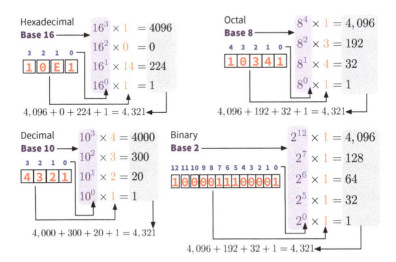

Figure 8.1   The number 4,321 in different bases.

II   Cracking the Shift Cipher

In the "Secret Code 😟" problem of sec. 3.1, we challenged you to crack the substitution cipher that encrypted the following message:

```
MAXI KBVX HYLX VNKB MRBL XMXK GTEO BZBE TGVX VTKX
EXLL VHFF NGBV TMBH GLVH LMEB OXL
```

One simple approach is to try all possible number of shifts on the first few letters of the ciphertext:

```
LZWH JAUW  KYVG IZTV  JXUF HYSU              NBYJ LCWY
  ↑↑↑          ↑↑↑         ↑↑↑                  ↑↑↑
   1            2           3        · · ·       25
MAXI KBVX  MAXI KBVX  MAXI KBVX              MAXI KBVX
```

This is a decent way to find the solution, but with a pen and paper we can go a bit faster. First, take the first letter of the ciphertext and write down the rest of the alphabet backwards, like so:

```
1 2 3 · · · · · · · · · · · · · · · · · · · ·25
M L K J I H G F E D C B A Z Y X W V U T S R Q P O N
```

Notice that after arriving at the letter A, we continue counting from the last letter of the alphabet: Z,Y,Z.... Let's add more lines of the reversed alphabet, each time starting with the next letter of the ciphertext:

```
1 2 3 · · · · · · · · · · · · · · · · · · ·25
M L K J I H G F E D C B A Z Y X W V U T S R Q P O N
A Z Y X W V U T S R Q P O N M L K J I H G F E D C B
```

```
1 2 3 · · · · · · · · · · · · · · · · · · ·25
M L K J I H G F E D C B A Z Y X W V U T S R Q P O N
A Z Y X W V U T S R Q P O N M L K J I H G F E D C B
X W V U T S R Q P O N M L K J I H G F E D C B A Z Y
```

```
1 2 3 · · · · · · · · · · · · · · · · · · ·25
M L K J I H G F E D C B A Z Y X W V U T S R Q P O N
A Z Y X W V U T S R Q P O N M L K J I H G F E D C B
X W V U T S R Q P O N M L K J I H G F E D C B A Z Y
I H G F E D C B A Z Y X W V U T S R Q P O N M L K J
```

Can you see a pattern emerge in a column? Let's continue for a few more lines:

```
  1 2 3 · · · · · · · · · · · · · · ·19· · · · ·25
M L K J I H G F E D C B A Z Y X W V U T S R Q P O N
A Z Y X W V U T S R Q P O N M L K J I H G F E D C B
X W V U T S R Q P O N M L K J I H G F E D C B A Z Y
I H G F E D C B A Z Y X W V U T S R Q P O N M L K J
K J I H G F E D C B A Z Y X W V U T S R Q P O N M L
B A Z Y X W V U T S R Q P O N M L K J I H G F E D C
V U T S R Q P O N M L K J I H G F E D C B A Z Y X W
X W V U T S R Q P O N M L K J I H G F E D C B A Z Y
```

The 19th column reads **THE PRICE**! Since all other columns are gibberish, we know we found our key:

```
A B C D E F G H I J K L M N O P Q R S T U V W X Y Z
                        19
                        ↓↓↓
D E F G H I J K L M N O P Q R S T U V W X Y Z A B C
```

We can now decrypt the entire text:

THEP RICE OFSE CURI TYIS ETER NALV IGIL ANCE CARE
LESS COMM UNIC ATIO NSCO STLI VES
                    ↑↑↑
                    19
MAXI KBVX HYLX VNKB MRBL XMXK GTEO BZBE TGVX VTKX
EXLL VHFF NGBV TMBH GLVH LMEB OXL

Finally, by rearranging the spaces and adding punctuation, we find:

THE PRICE OF SECURITY IS ETERNAL VIGILANCE.
CARELESS COMMUNICATIONS COST LIVES.

III   Cracking the Substitution Cipher

In the "Hollow Coin 🙂" problem of sec. 3.1, we challenged you to crack the substitution cipher that encrypted the following message:

```
DUA KVYBVHA PVJ OAZQMASAO DW CWES PQLA KASJWFVZZC.
AMASCDUQFH QJ VZZ SQHUD PQDU DUA LVGQZC. PA PQJU
CWE JEYYAJJ. HSAADQFHJ LSWG DUA YWGSVOAJ.
```

Let's start with the most basic frequency analysis observation: in English, the most common letter is E and the most common pair of consecutive letters is TH. Since the most common letter of the ciphertext is A and the most common letter pair is DU, we can try the mappings E→A and T,H→D,U:

```
THE KVYBVHE PVJ OEZQMESEO TW CWES PQLE KESJWFVZZC.
EMESCTHQFH QJ VZZ SQHHT PQTH THE LVGQZC. PE PQJH
CWE JEYYEJJ. HSEETQFHJ LSWG THE YWGSVOEJ.
```

Our work is made easier by the fact that the ciphertext has kept the spaces and punctuation of the plaintext. We can immediately see that our tentative mapping T,H,E→D,U,A has a good chance of being correct, as the common word THE appears three times!

Building on that assumption, there's a sentence that starts with PE, which could either stand for 'be', 'he' or 'we'. We already have a mapping for H, so we try B→P and W→P. The former takes us to a dead end: the sentence would then start with the phrase BE BQJH, which could only make sense if it stood for "be both", creating a conflict with our previous mapping T→D. Therefore, we retain W→P:

```
THE KVYBVHE WVJ OEZQMESEO TW CWES WQLE KESJWFVZZC.
EMESCTHQFH QJ VZZ SQHHT WQTH THE LVGQZC. WE WQJH
CWE JEYYEJJ. HSEETQFHJ LSWG THE YWGSVOEJ.
```

Let's have a look at the words with fewest missing letters. For instance, WQTH immediately gives us I→Q. With this new mapping, WQJH becomes WIJH, which in turn gives us S→J:

```
THE KVYBVHE WVS OEZIMESEO TW CWES WILE KESSWFVZZC.
EMESCTHIFH IS VZZ SIHHT WITH THE LVGIZC. WE WISH
CWE SEYYESS. HSEETIFHS LSWG THE YWGSVOES.
```

Again, we look for the words with fewest missing letters: WVS gives us A→V and TW gives us O→W. In addition, the fact an unknown character appears twice in the same word can also be a clue: SEYYESS gives us U,C→E,Y and HSEETIFHS gives us G,R,N→H,S,F:

THE KACBAGE WAS OEZIMEREO TO COUR WILE KERSWNAZZC. EMERCTHING IS AZZ RIGHT WITH THE LAGIZC. WE WISH COU SUCCESS. GREETINGS LROG THE COGRAOES.

The closer we get to the solution, the faster we advance! COUR and COU give us Y→C, EMERYTHING gives V→M, and EVERYTHING IS AZZ RIGHT gives us L→Z:

THE KACBAGE WAS OELIVEREO TO YOUR WILE KERSWNALLY. EVERYTHING IS ALL RIGHT WITH THE LAGILY. WE WISH YOU SUCCESS. GREETINGS LROG THE COGRAOES.

We're almost there! The missing mappings can quickly be resolved to P,K,D,F,O,M→K,B,O,L,W,G, and the plaintext holds no more secrets:

THE PACKAGE WAS DELIVERED TO YOUR WIFE PERSONALLY. EVERYTHING IS ALL RIGHT WITH THE FAMILY. WE WISH YOU SUCCESS. GREETINGS FROM THE COMRADES.

Finally, we can write down what we know of the encryption key, in case we find a new ciphertext that also uses it. The missing letters are those that don't appear in the message:

```
A B C D E F G H I J K L M N O P Q R S T U V W X Y Z
↓ ↓ ↓ ↓ ↓ ↓ ↓ ↓ ↓ ↓ ↓ ↓ ↓ ↓ ↓ ↓ ↓ ↓ ↓ ↓ ↓ ↓ ↓ ↓ ↓ ↓
E K Y T U N M G _ S P F V _ D W I _ R _ H A O _ C L
```

As you can see, this simple substitution cipher is not very secure, as we were able to crack it in a few straightforward steps. Although these ciphers are more challenging when the position of spaces is unknown, computers can make quick work of them regardless. To try that out, head over to http://code.energy/substitution.

IV Evaluating Classifiers

In Chapter 5, we learned about prediction models: algorithms that can make a series of predictions, which we call y, given data related to each prediction, which we call X. There are two types of models. Regressors make numerical predictions, while classifiers predict an outcome that's divided into labeled groups. We already learned to score how well a regressor is making its predictions. Let's now learn how to score classifers as well.

Since classifiers predict labels, let's start simple: suppose y is made of binary data. Since it has only *two labels*, all we need is a yes or no answer for each row. We call this **binary classification**. Predicting if a patient will develop diabetes or if a credit card purchase is fraudulent are examples of binary classification.

A natural approach is to evaluate the percentage of correct predictions, called the **accuracy**. However, this is often a terrible way to assess how well a model is doing. Let's see how it fares:

> FINDING FRAUD 💳 You're the techie of a bank trying to prevent credit card fraud. They asked you to create a model that predicts if a payment is fraudulent based on transaction details. You trained two models—a *chilled model* 😎 and a *paranoid model* 😱—to predict fraud on exisiting data of 1,000 transactions, of which 10 are known cases of fraud. You now wish to compare their performance to an untrained *lazy model* 😴 that randomly calls 1% of transactions fraudulent. Here is how each of the three models performed:
>
> 😴 Found no fraud, incorrectly called 10,
> 😎 Found 8 frauds, incorrectly called 19 more,
> 😱 Found all frauds, incorrectly called 87 more.
>
> Which model is most accurate?

The paranoid model missed no frauds, therefore it made $0+87=87$ mistakes and 913 correct predictions, yielding an accuracy of 91.3%.

The chilled model missed 2 frauds, therefore it made $2+19=21$ mistakes and 979 correct predictions, yielding an accuracy of 97.9%. On the other hand, the lazy model missed the 10 frauds, therefore it made $10+10=20$ mistakes and 980 correct predictions, yielding an accuracy of 98%. The lazy model is the most accurate, even though it's useless!

To better evaluate classifiers, we must see *how* they make right and wrong predictions. To this end, we build a **confusion table** that counts correct and incorrect predictions for each label:

	Predicted	
	Fraud (10)	No Fraud (990)
Fraud (10)	0	10
No Fraud (990)	10	980

	Predicted	
	Fraud (27)	No Fraud (973)
Fraud (10)	8	2
No Fraud (990)	19	971

	Predicted	
	Fraud (97)	No Fraud (903)
Fraud (10)	10	0
No Fraud (990)	87	903

	Predicted	
	Fraud (10)	No Fraud (990)
Fraud (10)	10	0
No Fraud (990)	0	990

Figure 8.2 Confusion tables for the lazy, chilled, and paranoid classifiers. A *unicorn* 🦄 classifier with 100% accuracy is shown for reference.

A prediction is incorrect when the predicted label and the true label differ, as shown in red in fig. 8.2. Notice how the previously mentioned accuracies can be obtained for each table by dividing the sum of black cells by 1,000. Let's now see which other metrics we can use to make sense of the confusion tables.

SENSITIVITY The percentage of fraud that a model is able to identify is the **sensitivity score**. For example:

- 😴 Found 0 of 10 frauds, sensitivity = 0%,
- 😎 Found 8/10 frauds, sensitivity = 80%,
- 🙀 Found 10/10 frauds, sensitivity = 100%.

Here, the best sensitivity score is obtained by the paranoid model, since it was able to identify the complete list of frauds. On the other hand, the chilled model found most frauds, but the list was incomplete. The lazy model was the least sensitive, since it found nothing interesting!

PRECISION The percentage of a model's predictions of fraud which are correct is the **precision score**. For example:

- 😴 Correct about 0 of 10 predicted frauds, precision = 0%,
- 😎 Correct about 8/27 predicted frauds, precision ≈ 29.6%,
- 🙀 Correct about 10/97 predicted frauds, precision ≈ 10.3%.

The best precision score was obtained by the chilled model, since almost a third of the predicted frauds were actual frauds. The paranoid model is less precise: only 10% of them are useful. Finally, the lazy model was the least precise, since all of its fraud predictions are useless!

It is now clear that the lazy model is terrible. However, it can be difficult to choose which is better between the chilled and the paranoid models, since one has better sensitivity and the other has superior precision. Thankfully, there is a commonly used metric that solves this issue.

F₁ SCORE A good evaluation of a model's predictive performance considers both sensitivity and precision. If either is zero, the model has no predictive power, so its final score should also be equal to zero. To achieve this, scientists calculate a special kind of average (called the *harmonic mean*) on the sensitivity and precision scores. They call it the **F₁ score**:

$$F_1 = 2 \times \frac{\text{precision} \times \text{sensitivity}}{\text{precision} + \text{sensitivity}}.$$

The F_1 score ranges from 0 to 1 (or 100%). Plugging the precision and sensitivity scores in the formula for each model, we find:

- 😓 $F_1 = 0\%$,
- 😎 $F_1 \approx 0.43 = 43\%$,
- 😋 $F_1 \approx 0.19 = 19\%$.

According to this metric, the chilled model has more than twice the predictive power than the paranoid model. This stems mainly from the paranoid model's terrible precision.

FALSE ALARMS From a customer's perspective, there's one more important metric: how often will my honest transactions get rejected? The percentage of truly good transactions that were incorrectly classified as fraud is called the **false alarm rate**, also known as the **false positive rate**. For instance:

- 😓 Incorrect about 10 of 990 honest transactions, FAR $\approx 1.0\%$,
- 😎 Incorrect about 19/990 honest transactions, FAR $\approx 1.9\%$,
- 😋 Incorrect about 87/990 honest transactions, FAR $\approx 8.8\%$.

Here, the paranoid model distinguishes itself from the others by raising many false alarms: nearly one in ten honest transactions are classified as fraud. Depending on the application, the false alarm rate is used instead of the precision in order to quantify a model's usefulness.

When evaluating your model, try to formulate what your are calculating in a sentence rather than with math only. In our example, we could say: *"the paranoid model blocked 8.8% of transactions by honest clients."* This can help you choose which metrics matter the most in your specific situation.

Classification Trade-Off

A classifier's `predict` function outputs the label it believes each row is most likely to assume. In addition, most classifiers can provide its estimation of the *probability* that a row belongs to a label. This way, we can change a model's label assignment logic to predict a label more often. This technique allows us to obtain two seemingly very different models from a single engine:

y		y_pred	
True Label	Pred. Fraud Probability	0.50 threshold	0.30 threshold
No Fraud	0.05	No Fraud	No Fraud
Fraud	0.55	Fraud	Fraud
No Fraud	0.39	No Fraud	Fraud
No Fraud	0.48	No Fraud	Fraud
No Fraud	0.17	No Fraud	No Fraud
No Fraud	0.33	No Fraud	Fraud
Fraud	0.31	No Fraud	Fraud

😎

		Predicted	
		Fraud (1)	No Fraud (6)
Truth	Fraud (2)	1	1
	No Fraud (5)	0	5

😱

		Predicted	
		Fraud (3)	No Fraud (4)
Truth	Fraud (2)	2	0
	No Fraud (5)	3	2

Figure 8.3 Classifying using two different thresholds.

By setting a lower threshold, the model is more sensitive to clues for fraud, so sensitivity gets a boost. On the other hand, more purchases are incorrectly classified as fraudulent, thwarting precision.

Since the precision, sensitivity, and F_1 scores change according to the threshold, a single measurement of these scores isn't sufficient to comprehensively evaluate a classifier. In our small sample, the higher threshold yields $F_1 \approx 0.67$, whereas the lower threshold yields $F_1 \approx 0.57$. However, this doesn't necessarily indicate the higher threshold is preferable.

Choose your evaluation method and classifier threshold according to real world needs. If the benefit of identifying fraud is high, and the downside of incorrectly classifying valid purchases is low, the higher threshold may be better.

In general, we try to assess the minimal acceptable sensitivity and precision scores early. If other people are going to use our classifier, they should help determine the bounds of the trade-off for adjusting the threshold.

ROC Curves

The early-warning radar was a brand new technology at the onset of World War II. Radars sometimes picked up signals which puzzled its operators. They weren't always sure if faint signals came from enemy aircraft or from parasitic radio noise, yet they had to decide whether to raise the alarm. A false alarm wasted precious resources, but ignoring a real threat could have devastating consequences.

While trying to determine which radio signals were true threats, a radar operator worked similarly to a classifier. The metrics used to score classifiers also work to gauge radar performance: the sensitivity is the percentage of incoming enemy aircraft that triggered an alarm, and the false alarm rate is the percentage of non threatening radio signals that triggered an alarm.

Radar operators quickly realized there was a trade-off between the sensitivity and false alarm rate. Sensitivity could be boosted by making radio receivers register weaker signals, but doing so also made it trigger more false alarms. To decide how sensitive their radio receivers should be, they decided to collect data at many different settings and plot the resulting scores:

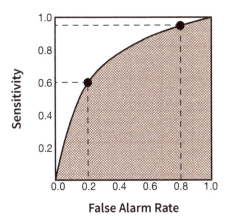

Figure 8.4 If this old radar was tuned to detect 95% of invading aircraft, about 80% of non-threatening radio signals resulted in false alarms. Making the receiver less sensitive reduced the false alarm rate to 20%, but in doing so, only 60% of incoming aircraft could be detected.

They called it a receiver operating characteristic (**ROC**) curve. Radars were then improved and delivered higher sensitivity for the same false-alarm rate, and ROC curves moved upwards on their plots. In general terms, the better the radar technology, the larger the shaded area under the curve (**AUC** score) shown in fig. 8.4.

You can plot a ROC curve for your own classifier by calculating the sensitivity and false-positive rate for all possible classification thresholds. The curve can help you decide which threshold to use.

Also, the AUC score is a good indicator of the classifier's overall performance. This score is useful as a generic assessment of predictive power, especially if you haven't yet chosen which threshold you'll use with the classifier.

Multiclass Classification

Scores for binary classifiers can also be adapted for classifying more than two labels. For instance, suppose you have to guess whether a person is born in the US, Mexico, or Canada. You train a classifier, and then try it with 100 people: 65 Americans, 25 Mexicans, and 10 Canadians. Prediction results can be summarized in a 3-by-3 confusion table, so we can see *how* predictions were right or wrong for each label:

		Predicted		
		🇺🇸 (51)	🇲🇽 (37)	🇨🇦 (12)
Truth	🇺🇸 (65)	39	24	2
	🇲🇽 (25)	11	13	1
	🇨🇦 (10)	1	0	9

Figure 8.5 Confusion table of a multiclass classifier.

The table shows where the model is confused. It had a difficult time differentiating 🇺🇸 and 🇲🇽 : Americans were incorrectly classified as Mexicans 24 times, and Mexicans were incorrectly classified as Americans 11 times. This suggests that more features with clues to distinguish Americans from Mexicans should be added.

The diagonal of black numbers contains the correct guesses. The model was correct 39+13+9=61 times out of 100, so its accuracy is 61%. As we've seen, accuracy can be misleading, and we must use metrics such as sensitivity and precision in order to capture a model's true predictive power. Since these metrics are defined for binary classification, we must re-express our multiclass classifier as a combination of binary classifiers:

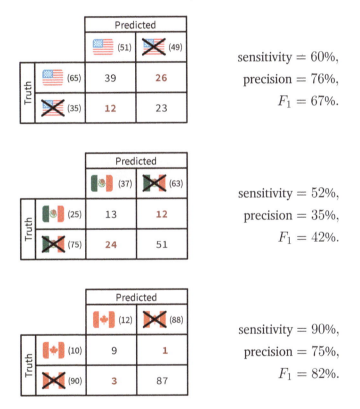

Figure 8.6 A multiclass classifier seen as three binary classifiers. For each label, a confusion table is built where all other labels were grouped. For instance, the first confusion table shows how the model classified people as American or non-American.[1] With this trick, we can calculate precision, sensitivity, and F_1 for each label.

---

[1]If the output y_{pred} is one-hot encoded, each of these confusion tables corresponds to one of the one-hot encoded columns.

In order to obtain a single score for the model, we calculate the mean of the three individual F_1 scores, which is 0.64. This is called the **macro F_1 score**. However, this score can be unfair: the 🇨🇦 label contributes to the macro score as much as the 🇺🇸 label, even though there are over six times more 🇺🇸 labels. When averaging label scores, it's best to calculate a *weighted* mean, where each weight is the count of a label in y. We call it the **micro F_1 score**:

$$\frac{(65 \times 0.67) + (25 \times 0.42) + (10 \times 0.82)}{65 + 25 + 10} \approx 0.62 = 62\%.$$

Make sure you see in fig. 8.6 where each of the numbers 65, 25, and 10 come from. Moreover, remember these scores only represent the performance of the model for the specific label thresholds you are using, as seen for binary classifiers. If you adjust the thresholds, the same model will yield different scores.

INDEX

MORE FROM CODE ENERGY

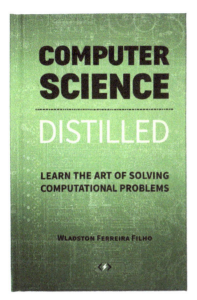

In this book, we explore how computer science has radically changed the way we exchange information and learn from large amounts of data, but we don't examine how the computers themselves work and how coders interact with them. This is because we already cover the core concepts of computer science in our first book, **Computer Science Distilled**. We strongly recommend you check it out!

Computer Science Distilled is a brief walk-through of essential computer science concepts you must know. Its writing style is similar to *Computer Science Unleashed*: academic formalities are kept to a minimum, and the language is clear and accessible. The book was also designed for beginners.

It starts with a light introduction to discrete mathematics and then presents common algorithms and data structures. Finally, it outlines the working principles of computer hardware and programming languages. Understanding these topics is your next step to computer science mastery, as they neatly complement the content of this book. Get your copy of **Computer Science Distilled** at:

http://code.energy/computer-science-distilled

COLOPHON

This book was created with X̲ǝLATEX, a type-setting engine for Donald Knuth's TEX system. The text is set Charter, a typeface designed by Matthew Carter in 1987, based on Pierre-Simon Fournier's characters from the XVIII Century. Other fonts include **Source Code Pro**, Source Sans Pro and CALENDAS PLUS.

The emoji 😜 were kindly provided by Twemoji, an open-source project maintained by Twitter.

The cover image was created from schematics of the first electronic computers, built between 1941 and 1945: Zuse's Z3, Turing's Colossus, Harvard's Mark I, and the ENIAC.